WHERE YOU GO, I WILL GO

LESSONS FROM A MILITARY SPOUSE

VICTORIA TERRINONI

This book is dedicated to my husband, Dave. I told you I would follow you to the ends of the earth, but I did not know you would take me up on it! Thank you for the extraordinary journey. I love you.

"Where you go, I will go, and where you stay, I will stay."

— Book of Ruth 1:16, www.Biblegateway.com

TABLE OF CONTENTS

INTRODUCTION

The boss's dog died on our watch. In fact, the dog passed the first night we were caring for her. The boss let us stay in his house in exchange for us watching his aging dog, Gigi. We took real good care of her. What an introduction to military life. My husband, Dave, was a chaplain candidate that fateful summer of 1987. He was not even on active duty yet, and things were already going wrong. Things did get better over his 31-year Air Force career, but it was not without its hardships.

As a new military spouse, you are no doubt confused and maybe a little bit afraid of this lifestyle you are embarking on. I know I was. At times I felt alone and lonely. Even the mention of moving could send me into a tizzy. And deployments? Ugh.

First and foremost, please know you are NOT alone. Each year, 150,000 men and women join the military with about half joining the enlisted corp. Currently, there are approximately 1.2 million active-duty spouses. With few exceptions, these spouses also had more questions than answers in the beginning, but they took a leap of faith anyway.

I had no idea what was in store for me. I told Dave once that I would follow him to the ends of the earth, but I never thought he'd take me up on that offer. When we married in 1982, neither the ministry nor the military was in our future plans. But when our twin daughters were six weeks old, Dave felt a strong calling to become a minister. I'll never forget the moment. Our twins were asleep, and I was lounging and reading on our couch when he came downstairs and told me he thought he was being called to be a minister. As I lowered my magazine, I said, "You'll make a wonderful minister. I will make a horrible minister's wife."

You see, I was raised Roman Catholic. Although we attended a Presbyterian Church, our minister's wife was my first role model. They had no children to chase after. She played the piano, sang and led the choir, and was superintendent of Sunday school. I did none of those things, and I had just given birth to twins.

For several months, Dave came home wondering why he was at the seminary. Dave knew he was being called to the ministry, and the seminary was the right place for him, but he hadn't found his gifts yet. Dave did say he didn't want to preach. Ironic since he won the school's preaching award when he graduated.

One day, in the middle of his third quarter in the fall of 1986, Dave came home all excited.

"I know why I am in seminary now," he said. That day, he met an Air Force Chaplain. "That's what I want to do." The rest was history.

I felt at peace with both the decision to go to seminary and the Air Force idea. We spent the next four years getting Dave through school and checking off all the right boxes to get him into the Air Force. They even brought him in a year earlier than expected. I should have known then how his career would affect my journalism career because I just assured my bosses I would be staying at the newspaper for another year. They gave me a promotion I'd been working toward for the past year. One week later to the day, Dave got called onto active duty. I couldn't ask him to delay going in after all the hoops the Air Force went through to offer him the active-duty slot early in the first place. Plus, this was the thing we'd been working toward for several years.

And so, together we started our military journey, having more questions than answers. But we made that leap of faith and never turned back.

Military life is hard, but it is also fantastic. Most of my closest friendships came about because of shared military experiences. I learned how to be independent and robust and that it is okay to ask for help if you need it. Most of all, I learned to embrace military life in all its forms -- the good, the bad, and the change it brings with each move.

If you feel this way, this book is written for you. Through personal experience, I will show you how to survive the bad -- deployments -- and love the good -- friends. After 31 years as an Air Force spouse and having moved 14 times for his various assignments, I have heard and seen many things about the service: good and bad. Although my stories are gleaned from my life in the Air Force, I feel the issues are the same across all branches of service.

I know you have questions about what this military lifestyle is all about. I will address the most-often-asked questions, help you to navigate through unfamiliar terms and protocols, give you some insight so you can find your place in the military family, and show you how to get the most out of your life as an armed-forces spouse. Seasoned spouses will enjoy the memories my stories evoke and may have more to add.

Turn the page and let us begin this journey together, starting with the story of Gigi.

PART 1: THE BEGINNING

In the summer of 1987, Dave packed his bags for the first time and left for a two-and-a-half-month stay at Pease Air Force Base in New Hampshire, where he served as a chaplain candidate in the Air Force Chaplain Candidate program. The program allowed seminary students to "try out" the military for two summer tours as Second Lieutenants. If at the end of the program the candidate decided the military was not for them, they can decommission and owe nothing to the military. It is a good deal for all parties involved.

CHAPTER 1: THE STORY OF GIGI

Dave and I had never been apart for longer than a weekend in our five years of marriage. So, our twin girls and I flew to New Hampshire to spend the Fourth of July week with him. The wing chaplain, Dave's boss, offered his house and car to us while he and his family were on vacation. We only needed to take care of their aging dog, Gigi. The boss said Gigi was old, and the family knew she would not be long for this world. That day surely would be a sad day for the family.

Our first day with Gigi went just fine. The girls, who were 18 months old, loved Gigi -- the first time they ever liked a dog. She was a sweet, old girl in a roly-poly body, probably because she would only eat hot dogs, lots of hot dogs! That night, as we got ready for bed, Dave let Gigi out to do her business before retiring for the evening.

Like many old mammals, including humans, Gigi could not hold her bladder for long. About 4:30 in the morning, she wanted to go out again. Dave grumbled all the way to the back door to let her out. Since the boss lived on a large rural property, Dave left Gigi outside. But Gigi kept barking and barking, so Dave, grumbling again, went to let her back in. He called her name. All he heard was "yip, yip" and then a high-pitched "YELP."

"GIGI!" he screamed. Then he stormed into the bedroom.

"What's going on?" I asked.

"An animal just grabbed Gigi," he said, finding his shoes, his robe, and the BB gun that was in the bedroom.

"What do you mean an animal grabbed Gigi?"

"I saw two eyes glowing and Gigi hanging from an animal's mouth."

Gigi had an overweight beagle body mounted on dachshund legs. She waddled when she walked. What animal could grab her?

"Well, what was it?"

"I don't know, but I'm going to go see if I can find it," said Dave. So, my brave 150-pound husband, in his robe and shoes, holding a BB gun, walked the perimeter of the property looking for a wild animal who just carried off a dog. Probably not the best idea.

Soon, Dave returned. "I think we better call the police," he said and went off to do that. Meanwhile, I threw on some clothes. Shortly, a police cruiser arrived, then a second from the nearby town, then a third.

"We heard it on the radio. We couldn't believe it, so we came to see what happened," one of the cops said, while the others seemed to be trying to hide their laughter at the sight of my husband -- robe, shoes, BB gun, and all.

The cops decided it was probably a fox. They could not do anything, so they left, and Dave and I went back to bed.

The next morning was a roller coaster of emotion. We got a call from the base chapel. A neighbor found Gigi in his yard, and miraculously she was still alive. The neighbor, knowing whose dog she was, rushed her to the vet. Our hearts soared. She was still alive. Of course, our girls, for the first time in their short lives, woke up and immediately started asking for Gigi. Great! They finally like a dog, and now this happens.

We drove to the chapel to find any contact information for the wing chaplain. When we arrived, news came that Gigi died on the operating table. What a way to start our new military life! Maybe we should not follow this avenue after all since now we have to call Dave's new boss and tell him what happened. The chapel did not have any vacation contact for him though. Dave called the vet, and we went back to the house.

We knew the boss was visiting family in one of the Carolinas. As a journalist who worked for several newspapers over the years, I went into my investigative-reporter mode and snooped through drawers and other places until I found an address book. In the book was a group with the same last name living in the Carolinas. It was worth a shot, so Dave started calling people on the list, all the time praying the boss would answer the phone and not one of the kids. No such luck. The teenage daughter answered. "Did something happen to Gigi?" she asked. Well, makes sense, I guess, because why else would we be calling?

"Well, sweetheart, Gigi died today," Dave said.

The daughter's reply. "Okay, thanks," and she hung up.

The boss called back when he got the news. He told Dave to bury Gigi's body somewhere on the property and not tell him where she was buried. He thanked us for calling. Dave retrieved Gigi's remains from the vet, who had frozen the body until arrangements could be made for either cremation or burial. So, to say the least, I was surprised to see him carry a mummy-wrapped, dog-sized bundle through the house and then put it in the freezer.

"What are you doing?" I asked, too shocked to actually say out loud, "You are NOT seriously putting that in there with our food, are you?"

Dave had planned to keep her in the freezer until he could dig a hole on the property as instructed. But when he tried to dig, the ground was rock solid, and he could not dig deep enough to bury the dog. After discussing what to do next, Dave took Gigi out of the freezer, back to the veterinarian's office, and paid him $15 to bury Gigi.

We tried to enjoy the rest of our vacation at a quaint bed and breakfast in North Conway, New Hampshire, feeling horrible that Gigi had died on our watch.

At the end of the week, the girls and I flew home to Illinois, and Dave followed at the end of August. After dropping Dave off at the airport, the boss gave Dave $15 to cover Gigi's burial. "Next time, you might want to get the receipt," the boss said. "The vet called and said you forgot it."

The saga of Gigi followed us for years afterward. In 1988, while at a conference in Colorado, Dave was walking by a group of chaplain candidates and heard one say, "The guy at Pease before me killed the boss's dog." Dave stuck his head in the group and said, "Yes, and it was the worst day of my life." And several years later, as he was walking through an airport in France, Dave heard a voice say, "Sure, you kill a guy's dog and then don't even stop to say hello," his former boss said.

Gigi may be dead and buried, but she will live in our hearts, minds, and memories for the rest of our lives.

Lessons Learned:

• *Flexibility, flexibility, flexibility, which by the way is the "f" word in our house. Things are going to happen. Go with the flow.*

• *Learn to see the humor in everything. Laughing at yourself is a lifesaver!*

CHAPTER 2: CHAPLAIN CANDIDATE PROGRAM -- THE SECOND YEAR

The following summer, the girls and I joined Dave for his Chaplain Candidate Program at Hurlburt Field, Florida. Hurlburt Field is next to Eglin Air Force Base on the Florida Panhandle. What a great place to experience military life! It has some of the most beautiful beaches in the world, crystal-clear blue Gulf of Mexico waters, and there are seafood restaurants everywhere. Not bad for my trial run of military life.

But paradise did not last long. The lodging office made a mistake and put Dave in a single room with a kitchenette shared with the room next door. They did not get the word Dave was bringing his family, and by that time no family units were available. So, we spent two-and-a-half months with two 2-year-olds in a single room. To top it off, in the Florida Panhandle during the summer months, it rains at least once a day so we could not go outside much of the time to escape our cramped quarters.

One day, when we did make it to the nearest playground, Dave called to tell us to stay out of the playground because a giant alligator was prowling around the area. Welcome to Florida, kids. No more swings for us until I felt suffocated in the room again.

To cope with being cooped up most of the time with my toddlers, I found I had to change my name. Hearing "Mommy, Mommy" all day long tried my patience to the very last nerve, so one day, I told the girls my name was not Mommy. It was Aunt Frieda. And they called me Aunt Frieda for the rest of our time in Florida. It was a little hard to explain to visitors, but it was funny and somehow less irksome than hearing Mommy all the time.

Despite the room situation, I really enjoyed our time in Florida. I learned a lot about a military spouse's role in the Air Force and had a lot of fun with all the social activities. The vice wing commander's wife, Phoebe, took me under her wing and helped me navigate the social aspects of being a military spouse. She also helped me to find a babysitter so I could participate in all the various functions.

One Sunday evening, while having dinner at Phoebe's house, I was mortified when the girls stripped naked in her living room. Phoebe showed me how to handle the situation with grace and tact. She marched them down to the bathroom and gave the girls a bath. I wanted to be just like her when I got to be a Colonel's wife.

Despite all I learned that summer, I still made mistakes, but thankfully nothing too earth-shattering. Very few things a spouse does will affect the military member's job unless it is really egregious.

Commissaries Have Lines?

One of those mistakes happened during my first visit to the base commissary. I thought I hit the jackpot because there was no one in line at any open registers. I chose one and started unpacking my cart. "The line starts back here," I heard an annoyed voice announce behind me. I turned around, and sure enough, five or six people were lined up down the aisle behind me. Commissaries have grocery line protocols. Who knew? I reloaded my cart and, red-faced, walked to the end of the line, mumbling my apologies all the way down the aisle.

Although it may look like a regular grocery store, do not let a military commissary fool you. They have just as many protocols as the rest of the military. Commissaries are grocery stores that serve military families at a discount. They generally are cheaper than grocery stores in town and do not charge tax, although a five-percent surcharge is added to each bill. The commissary is excellent for picking up the essential items, plus if you live on base, they are nearby. However, if you need an item that is a little out of the ordinary, they probably won't have it.

But they have rules of engagement, such as the line you wait in until called to the next available cashier. At that time when I was a new military spouse, the line for the cashier went down one of the aisles, but that sometimes made it hard for shoppers to get items off the shelf. Now, they have roped-off areas like the ones used at airport security checkpoints. You still wait for the next available cashier, but at least now you know where to stand.

Also, at that time, commissaries had arrows directing traffic up and down aisles. Those, too, are gone now, which is a good thing since no one paid any attention to them anyway.

The other mistake most new spouses make is not tipping the bagger. Unlike civilian stores, baggers in commissaries work for tips only. They are usually spouses, retirees, and high school students. They do not make great money, so please remember to tip them.

Also, do not go to the commissary on payday. It seems the entire base is there at that time, and it also seems those are the days they only have a few checkout lanes open. On paydays, the lines can back up into the aisles, even with the cattle chute used to maintain lines.

Once you learn to navigate around people parking their cart in the middle of the aisle, or try to avoid those people revealing all their private business loudly on their cell phone, the commissary really is worth the savings in both time and money.

How to Address a Senior Officer

It seems I made most of my mistakes the summer we were at Hurlburt. By the time Dave officially joined the military, protocols had relaxed a little, but they were still strict. At Hurlburt Field in 1988, wives wearing white gloves to social events and carrying calling cards were (thankfully!) on the way out. But like all cultural shifts, it takes one generation to complete the change started by their predecessors. Until the older generation retires, some long-held customs will not wholly die away. I learned one of these protocols -- how to address a senior officer -- the hard way.

Let me just say here that I did not completely embarrass myself. My faux pas only seemed abhorrent to a few older spouses. But it did change my way of thinking and speaking in public.

When we arrived at Hurlburt Field, Dave was a second lieutenant, the officer corps' lowest rank. The vice wing commander, the second in command at a base, and his wife took our family under their wing, showing us around and having us over for dinner. They were Presbyterian and had never had a Presbyterian chaplain before on base, so they adopted us, making us feel welcomed. Shortly after meeting them for the first time, we were at an official party, and I saw Scott. Scott was a colonel, one rank below the generals. As I passed him, he said hello to me.

"Hi, Scott. How are you?" I replied quickly. I heard gasps behind me.

"You do not address a colonel by his first name," a woman said.

Oh no! Did I just kill my husband's career? Would my mistake get Dave in trouble? Back in those days, a wife's actions could reflect poorly on the military spouse. Today, minor errors, like calling a colonel by their first name, will not get your military member kicked out. You must murder someone, harm your children, or be a drug mule for that to happen. I quickly sought out the Colonel's wife to see how I could undo the damage.

"Phoebe, I just called Scott by his first name. Did I do something wrong?"

"How did he introduce himself to you?" she said.

"As Scott."

"Then he wants you to call him Scott. Don't worry about it," she replied.

Phew, I had not ruined Dave's career, but even today, I still have trouble calling a general by his first name, unless his first name happens to be Sir.

Lessons Learned:

- *You will make mistakes and feel like a fool sometimes. Use them as learning opportunities and don't worry. You have not ruined your spouse's career!*
- *Trust me... Someday you will laugh about those incidents and retell those stories to others so they can laugh, too.*

PART 2:
PCS: MILITARY SPEAK FOR MOVING

Permanent Change of Station, or PCS, is what the military calls a move from one base to another. It is different from temporary duty assignments (TDY) and deployments, usually involving the military member going away without family only for a while. When it is a PCS and the family also is moving, the military *tries* to make it as stress-free as possible. But is it? The movers are hired by the service to pack up all your household goods, load them on a truck, drive them to your new location, and unload the moving van. They will even unpack boxes if you want them to.

Why would that be stressful? You just have to sit around and wait until the house is empty and then clean the house to pass inspection before you leave, right? Hah!

First, the movers bid on moves, and usually, the lowest bidder gets the contract. Second, they often are day workers with no experience in moving. And thirdly, they do not care about your stuff. Okay, I have had good movers, too, but just remember: it is not THEIR stuff. So instead of sitting around all day catching up on Netflix® before your television gets packed, you must watch them like a hawk. Even then, you will not catch everything. In the 14 moves I have made with the military, I cannot think of any PCS in which something did not go wrong.

My advice then? Stay on your toes, read all the paperwork, make all your special requests known, be prepared for the worst (see Chapter 3), and hopefully, you will be pleasantly surprised.

CHAPTER 3: MOVE TO GEORGIA

The year was 1992. We were about to embark on our first move into the military. We moved from northwest Illinois to Warner Robins Air Force Base in central Georgia. We did all the work ourselves in previous moves, so we had no idea what to expect from a moving company.

This is what to expect on each move:

1. The moving company sends someone to look at what you have so they can estimate the number and kind of boxes they will need, how many people to assign to the job, and how many days it should take.

2. The packers will come a day or two before the loaders (depending on how many days they have allotted) and pack up your stuff.

3 The loaders will come and load the truck and drive off to meet you at your new home.

This is what happened to us during our move to Georgia:

1. The driver showed up and did an inventory the day before, including items in our detached garage.

2. The same driver showed up the next day with his pre-teen son as his helper.

3. The driver forgot about our garage items.

4. The driver got angry about forgetting our garage items.

5. The driver literally crammed the last of our stuff on the truck and slammed the door, so it would not fall out.

6. The driver was at our house until well after midnight.

Being our first move, we did not know we could ask the driver to leave at 5 p.m. and come back the next day. My poor six-year-old girls slept on the empty living room floor until we finally left the house at 2 a.m.

We also did not know that our household goods would be put into a warehouse until we had a house where they could be delivered. The ideal move is door-to-door, but this is rare, especially if you are living on base. Once you get to your new location, you will probably be put up in a temporary lodging facility (TLF). Pray it is for a short time. When we arrived at Warner Robins, we were given a one-bedroom with a pullout couch in the living room. The wallpaper was peeling, and roaches were everywhere. Quite a welcome to this northern girl!

Luckily, Dave went to housing officials the first thing in the morning, and we were given a house. We were only in TLF for a weekend before our household goods arrived. You can borrow what is commonly known as "stick furniture," very basic furniture you might find in an inexpensive hotel, if you want to move into the house before your things are delivered. Most bases used to have loan closets for this purpose.

When our stuff arrived, we realized how stupid we were when packing up. There are many codes on the packing list you sign at both ends, one for pickup and one for delivery. As our goods were being delivered, I noticed all these codes on everything. When I looked at the codes' legend, I saw they indicated damage on *all* our items, including my brand-new, never-been-used washer and dryer.

I asked the Air Force's moving manager about all the codes. He noticed the damage marked on the dryer did not match the actual dent on the dryer, so we were able to file a claim for damages. But we learned a valuable lesson -- movers mark everything as damaged to lessen the amount that can be claimed. After that, we disputed markings on items *in writing* on the sheets before signing them.

Lessons Learned:

• *Learn what your rights are before the mover shows up.*

• *Keep your eye on the packing crew and don't sign anything until you make sure it is correct.*

• *Dispute anything marked on the sheets before letting the truck leave with your household goods. It will save a lot of hassles later if you have to file a claim.*

CHAPTER 4: NORTH BY NORTHWEST

I was walking with my Lakeside Walking Group one sunny February morning in Georgia. I had just returned from visiting Dave in Italy for 10 days. We knew we would move that summer, and after my trip to Italy, I went on and on about how I hoped our assignment would be to Italy, or at least Germany.

My friends exchanged looks. "Why are you guys looking at each other that way?" I asked.

"You don't know?"

"Know what?"

"You guys are moving to Eielson Air Force Base in Alaska. It was announced in chapel yesterday," they said.

This was the first time we heard anything about an assignment. I was angry that the chapel community was told before Dave or me. Usually, the commander informs the military member before telling anyone else. Apparently, the chapel staff was notified of impending moves. One chaplain took it upon himself to announce it to everyone during Sunday services.

When I got home from my walk, the first thing I did was call Dave. I knew he was flying, so I left a message with the base operations desk to ask Dave to call me back as soon as he could. "Tell him I know where we are going next," I said, knowing that would get him curious enough to call right away.

When Dave called, I broke the news. "We're going to Eielson in Alaska," I said.

News of new orders often takes a bit of time to digest, so Dave was quiet for a moment. Then he asked the usual questions -- how did I find out? Did I know our report date? And most importantly, how did I feel about it?

By this time, I had a few hours to think about it, and I was getting excited. Alaska! Who would not want to go there?

As soon as we hung up, I called my parents, who were excited as well. But Dave's mom, an eternal pessimist, broke down and cried. "What did you do to deserve this?" she choked out. Finally, she calmed down after I explained it was a good thing.

I hung up the phone and began to research everything I could about the base and the Fairbanks area.

When the Military Member Is Not Home to Make the Move

Dave was home from Italy for a week when he went on a weeklong temporary duty assignment, or TDY, while we were still living in Georgia. He was not home much of our third year at Warner Robins between TDYs, exercises, and his deployment to Italy. He was gone so much the girls started calling him the guest. While on this latest TDY, he learned he had been picked up for Squadron Officer School (SOS) at Maxwell Air Force Base (AFB) in Montgomery, Alabama. Dave would go to school en route to our assignment in Alaska.

It was a great honor to be picked up for SOS in residence, especially since he had already completed the distance-learning curriculum. SOS is the Air Force's primary development education program, offering captains the opportunity to learn required leadership skills and squadron operations to move up the ranks to major. At the time, only a certain number of captains were chosen to go through the training in person. We were honored by Dave's selection. The only problem was he would not be home to pack up the house. I was terrified of the prospect of doing it alone. Remember, my previous experience was the horrific move to Georgia.

Because Maxwell AFB is only four hours away from Warner Robins, Dave could arrange a few weekends home. We traded in both of our cars to buy a GMC Jimmy sport-utility vehicle for Alaska's winter conditions, so we only had one vehicle to drive around. A few weekends before the move, he put a cartop carrier on the Jimmy. He set aside a closet full of items he wanted to transport rather than giving them to the movers.

During the move, a neighbor helped me load the cartop carrier and the back of our SUV. But we had more than could fit, so I had to let the movers take some things. Apparently, I made the wrong decisions on what to let the mover have, and when Dave called on the last day of packing to see how everything was going, he indicated he was not happy that I let his flight helmet go with the movers.

"Well, I have my seat and two seats open for the girls, and there is no room for you when we come to get you," I said. "Something is going to have to change if we are going to pick you up in Alabama."

Once we got to Alabama, we learned he was allowed to ship another 600 pounds of our stuff, but even then, we were crowded in that packed-to-the-gills SUV.

Cleaning House Should Not Be That Hard

The most stressful part of any move, especially if you live in a post or base housing, is getting out of the housing with all the military's checkboxes ticked off per its protocols. Before your packers come, a housing inspector shows up and gives you a long, detailed list of exactly what condition the house needs to be in when you move out. Never mind that the military gives you a 20-year-old home with the original appliances and carpet to begin with. You move in with all your belongings plus children and pets, yet the housing office expects it to look fresh when you leave. Impossible!

The cleaning list consists of tasks even a good housekeeper would not do, let alone someone like me who hates housework. We were lucky if I mopped the floors. Forget cleaning the seal around the dishwasher door. Who does that? In one move, the housing office even wanted the tops of the basement pipes to be dust-free. What?

Dave, being the smart man he is, opted to hire someone to clean for me. He knew I was already stressed from having to make this move by myself. Having to meet the inspector's requirements to clean the house would send me right over the edge. At that time, the housing office had a list of approved cleaners who did move-out cleaning, guaranteeing you would pass inspection. They were well worth the money. Now that most base housing is owned by private management companies, you can often pay a cleaning fee and walk away. Much easier.

The outside also needs to be neat and tidy. The lawn needs to be mowed and edged, the bushes trimmed, and the garden beds weeded. In Georgia, we had a big oak tree in our backyard with no grass at the trunk base. Nothing would grow because of the shade and sandy soil under the tree. We had tried to plant grass a few times, but it never took. At the pre-inspection, the inspector insisted that if I watered it, grass would grow. So, I did. At the inspection, the house passed, but the inspector asked about mud around the oak tree. "You told me to water, and I did," I said. They let it go.

Before leaving Georgia, the twins, Alanna and Marissa, and I spent a week in the base hotel so we could visit and say good-bye to friends. On our way out, we were at the Alabama border when we realized we had left a pillow but more importantly, we forgot Marissa's stuffed rabbit, Buns, in our room. Buns had been in the family since the girls' first Easter after they were born. She was special to our entire family. When I stopped for gas, I called Dave and told him what we had left behind. He called the lodging facility to alert them to this "urgent matter" and then called the chapel. One of the chaplains went to the lodging office, retrieved Buns, and shipped her to Illinois, where we would be stopping to visit family. All's well that ends well.

Another lesson learned -- do not leave anything behind, but if you do, it is good to have friends and coworkers you can rely on. This is truly the definition of "the military family." People who will go above and beyond to help you out.

North to Alaska

Once we picked up Dave in Alabama and watched him graduate from SOS, we made our way to Illinois to see our families. We knew we would see most of them the following summer when they came to visit, but that was a year away.

Nothing compared to the thrill of our first move to Alaska in 1995. What a magical time! We took our sweet time getting up to Alaska. Dave rigged a television with a VHS (yes, VHS) player on a box between the front bucket seats so our nine-year-old girls could watch videos if they got bored during the drive. We took 14 days to enjoy the beautiful landscape along the way through the upper States and western Canadian provinces.

Our most memorable stops included Glacier National Park in Montana, where we climbed on glaciers in our shorts! We also spent the night at a so-called "resort" in British Columbia, Canada, which were actually a bunch of tractor-trailers combined and renovated to make motel rooms. I did like this resort's signs that were friendly but in a passive-aggressive sort of way: "Don't use our towels to wash your car. Have a nice day." Smiley face. "If you steal our towels, we will call the RMPs (Royal Mounted Police). Have a nice day." Smiley face.

Another of our favorite stops was Mukluk Annie's Salmon Bake and Hotel along Teslin Lake in Teslin, Yukon Territory, Canada. In addition to the salmon bake, the restaurant offered boat rides on the beautifully smooth, crystal-clear lake.

We traveled the Alaska-Canada Highway built during World War II. It was and still is a famous drive for people who want to experience the untouched wilderness in northwest Canada and Alaska. Many small towns, mountains, and Dall sheep dot the landscape. You will also encounter moose, caribou, foxes, and, if you are lucky, a bear or two. In one small town, we ran into a family of four also going to Eielson. We struck up a friendship that lasted several years.

By taking our time, we bonded as a family. We saw breathtaking sights and never imagined the drive was just the beginning of the magic we would experience for three years.

Lessons Learned:

The physical act of moving is stressful. Do the best you can, take deep breaths, and look forward to the new adventure that awaits you.

If there is any family heirloom or prized possession that you would just die if it were to be damaged by the movers – TAKE IT WITH YOU!

CHAPTER 5: YOU WANT TO GO WHERE?

Every few years, you fill out what is called a "dream sheet" in the military. It is something used to let the powers-that-be know where you want to move to next. Actually, I think the assignments folks use them as comic relief.

For instance, every time we put down that we wanted to go to Europe, we got Alaska. I guess they figured Eielson and Europe both begin with an E, so what is the difference. It also seemed we got our third choice each time, except for Minot Air Force Base, North Dakota. When we put down Minot as our first choice, they willingly gave it to us.

Why Not Minot?

People thought we were crazy when we requested Minot Air Force Base, which is just south of the Canadian provinces of Saskatchewan and Manitoba. Minot was considered the Siberia of the Air Force. The common phrase was "Why not Minot?" The answer was "Freezin's the Reason." But honestly, we were coming from Fairbanks, Alaska. Minot's winters had nothing on the minus 50 temps in Fairbanks, without the windchill. The wind was the one thing Minot did have over Fairbanks. I often said it did not really snow in North Dakota; it just blew from Montana to Minnesota.

Before putting in our request, I remember the four of us sitting around the kitchen table discussing our next move. Where did we want to go? After making several suggestions, 12-year-old Alanna piped up and said, "What about Minot?" That got us thinking. One of our friends grew up in Minot and really liked it there. The airbase was small with a close-knit military community. Granted, they did not have the flashy F-16s or A-10s, but they flew the hefty B-52 bombers and maintained a large missile field. That could be cool.

The town of Minot was only 11 miles from the base as opposed to 25 for a trip into Fairbanks from Eielson base. And, Minot had three Dairy

Queens! The nearest Dairy Queen to Eielson at the time was in Seattle! That was a significant selling point for our DQ-loving family. Another bonus was its location closer to family in the Chicago area. After being 5,000 miles from our family while stationed in Alaska, Minot was an easy nine-hour drive down Interstate 94, which made it more convenient to be with our families when my grandfather died and after Dave's stepdad was diagnosed with colon cancer.

So, we put Minot as number one on our dream sheet. The assignments gurus could not believe it and called Dave three days in a row.

"Did you mean to put Minot as your first choice?" they asked.

"Yes, we did," Dave said.

The next day, "Are you sure you want Minot? We've penciled you in, but we want to make sure this is your request."

"Yes, it is," Dave said.

On the third day, they asked the question again. "You really meant to request Minot? Because it is yours, but you can change your mind."

Dave again replied that Minot was our wish. And so, it was decided: we were going to Minot.

When Dave got to his assignment, he learned all was not well there. Two chaplains had just been relieved of their duties after getting into some trouble. (Unfortunately, that happens sometimes.) A big shuffle took place, resulting in a new wing chaplain and another chaplain coming in to help pick up the pieces. What we learned was that Dave had been requested for this assignment specifically for his skills in working through such situations and fixing a broken staff.

Minot turned out to live up to our expectations. The only people who bad-mouthed Minot were those who never lived there. It was a great place to raise children with solid moral standards and values like our own. We felt we had stepped into the simpler times of the 1950s when we first arrived. Dave had to get some work done on our SUV, but the mechanic needed to order a part to fix it. He gave us the car back until the part came in but refused payment for the work he had already done. The mechanic trusted us to pay once the job was complete. We could not believe how much he trusted total strangers.

Minot Air Force Base was not without its troubles. When we drove onto the base the first time, we could feel a cloud of oppression over us. The evil vibe was palpable, and we were sure Satan had his hooks into that base, including the two chaplains who were relieved of their duties. In addition, First Lieutenant Kelly Flinn, the first female B-52 bomber pilot in the Air Force, had just been in the national spotlight after being discharged from the military because of an affair with the civilian husband of one of her subordinates at Minot. Flinn disobeyed a direct order from her commander to end the relationship and lied to him about doing so. Not an auspicious start for those of us who were new to this base. Minot AFB also made headlines several times since we left, like after a B-52 flew across the nation with a live nuclear weapon on board, or when several missileers were caught cheating on tests.

It was an uphill battle against the evil forces on that base for the chapel staff and us.

91st Space Wing Chaplain

Minot Air Force Base made up two nuclear triad arms in the U.S. with the 5th Bomb Wing and the 91st Space Wing. The bomb wing supported the B-52 Bombers capable of carrying nuclear bombs. The space wing handled 15 missile alert facilities (MAF) with 150 Minuteman III Intercontinental Ballistic Missiles (ICBM) scattered over 8,500 square miles in western North Dakota.

Dave served as the Space Wing Chaplain, which was perfect for him. Throughout his career, Dave most enjoyed visiting the troops. With an office in the Space Wing headquarters, airmen had easy access to him. His job also involved advising commanders on morale and ethics.

Because he liked visiting the troops where they work, traveling to the missile alert facilities became an issue because of the area's sheer size. The facilities were spread out over an 8,500-square-mile missile field. Dave wanted to visit these remote areas where some troops stayed for a week and others for 24-hour shifts. But driving to each MAF was time-consuming and could be dangerous in the winter months. Thus the "Chopper Chaplain" was born.

Dave came up with a plan. Pilots from the 54th Helicopter Squadron in the Space Wing needed flying hours each month, and Dave needed to get to the MAFs each month. Why couldn't the pilots get their hours in while flying him to the facilities? It was a win-win situation.

Word of this chaplain who flew in helicopters to visit the alert facilities spread quickly, partly because as a reporter for the Minot Daily News, I leaked the story. I did not write the story, though. That would have been a conflict of interest. Shortly after the article appeared in the newspaper, the local television station picked it up and filmed a segment. During a teaser about what was coming up, the news anchor called Dave the "Chopper Chaplain," and the nickname stuck. Dave was also featured on the Air Force News Network. It was all part of the creative and innovative ways Dave came up with in order to meet the spiritual and emotional needs of his troops.

And speaking of names, I apparently had a split personality when I was called Veronica, not Victoria, on two separate occasions in the same week. Because of Dave's position as the Space Wing Chaplain, I was listed twice in the Officers' Spouse Club directory. Once as Victoria and once as Veronica. I remember coming home from a luncheon and showing the directory to Dave.

"Who is this Veronica? And if she cleans, she can stay," I said.

Then a few days later, I went to the base pharmacy to pick up some prescriptions. When my medicine was ready, the pharmacist called out "Veronica Terrinoni." Again, I asked Dave, "Who is this Veronica?" I also added, "If she cleans, she can stay."

After that, my response became a long-standing joke. Several years later, when we were stationed in Mississippi, a Saudi Arabian Colonel offered to match Dave with a "good Saudi wife" because all imams have four wives. Dave told him he would ask me, and he was sure I would say, "If she cleans, she can stay." I did indeed say that, but the Saudi Colonel was not amused.

Minot Daily News

Minot turned out to be a very lucrative place for me. Before we even left Alaska, I was hired as a freelance writer for the Minot Daily News. They offered me a full-time position, but I wanted to stick with freelancing. I ended up working close to 40 hours a week anyway. I covered the Air Force Base and wrote other feature articles and some religious articles. It was a perfect fit. I do not think the base had such extensive coverage before I arrived or since I left.

I covered everything. I toured a missile alert facility and got a feel for life as a missile officer. I talked with aircraft maintenance to see what their jobs included. I was on hand when regular bombs for the B-52s were turned into smart bombs by attaching a guidance system that allowed for greater accuracy and less collateral damage. I taxied in a B-52 and learned about the capabilities of this massive plane. I flew on a helicopter and reported on its quick maneuverability and resulting air sickness from firsthand experience. I even got to sit in public policy meetings about the military with our U.S. Senator from North Dakota.

Reporting events on base requires working with the base's Public Affairs team. This was a good thing but challenging at times. As an officer's spouse, I quickly developed a relationship with the team because I did not have to be taught acronyms or other military-speak. Many people knew Dave, so most were receptive to talking with me.

The challenges included having to make interview appointments through Public Affairs and not make them on my own. Because I lived on base, I often found out about awards and other happenings before the Public Affairs office was ready to release them. For me, being able to scoop the television and radio stations in town was a bonus. But more often, I had to follow the Public Affairs lead and wait until they put out a press release. I am sure I drove them nuts sometimes, urging them to issue a press release before they were ready so I could get it in the paper.

I loved this job, and to this day, I am still friends with two of the Public Affairs officers and my editor at the Minot paper.

Lessons Learned:

• *Dream big on your dream sheet for where you want to be assigned next. You may actually get what you want. At the very least, you might give the assignment staff a chuckle!*

• *Don't forget to include your children in the decision-making process once they are old enough.*

CHAPTER 6: LIVING OFF BASE

If anyone told me I would fall in love with Montgomery, Alabama, I would have told them they were nuts. I do not like hot weather, nor am I a bug person, a sweat person, or a sweet-tea drinking person. But here we were. We moved to Maxwell Air Force Base in 2004, the week after the girls graduated high school, where Dave was attending Air Command and Staff College. I loved Alabama -- its history, the people, our church, jobs, and house.

Because Dave was there as a student for nine months, housing on base was limited. So, for the first time in his career, we lived off base. We rented the first year; a lovely, spacious ranch house with the most extensive kitchen I ever saw. But then we found out that Dave would be staying at Maxwell to teach at the Chaplain School for another two or three years, so we decided to buy a home. Property taxes were so low in Alabama, we could hardly afford not to purchase.

Building Our Dream House

The hunt for the right home can be tedious, but we agreed on what we were looking for -- a ranch-style home with a two-car garage and at least three bedrooms. Now for the where.

We rented in the village of Millbrook, about seven miles north of the base. We liked it there, but I really liked the town of Wetumpka, about 22 miles from the air force base. Dave did not want to live that far away. He also wanted a house with land and trees around it. We agreed we did not want to live in Montgomery itself.

We hired a real estate agent and started the hunt. Many houses in our price range were for sale, but none of them was what we wanted. I need neighbors, so I wanted a subdivision. Dave was okay with a subdivision if it was a little more rural. After driving around one day, I discovered the Summerfield Subdivision, about eight miles north of Millbrook. It fit all the criteria. We passed sheep, horses, and cows on the way to the subdivision, so Dave got his rural feel, and I got my neighborhood. Now to find the right house.

Dave and I drove around the neighborhood one Saturday just looking to see what was available. We found the perfect house at the end of a cul-de-sac with property backing up to a wooded area. It was what we were looking for, but we were hoping to park our travel trailer on the property too. We called the Realtor number on the sign and were told if the trailer were parked near the back of the site on a concrete pad, we would be allowed to keep it there. Score! This place was checking off a lot of boxes.

We called our Realtor, told her about the house, and asked her to set up an appointment to see it. Unfortunately, it sold before we could look at it. We also told her we wanted Summerfield, so she got to work. Most of the houses she showed us were okay, but none had the wow factor we were looking for. So, we finally settled on a place, but first we wanted to take measurements to ensure our furniture would fit. Then the unexpected happened.

"I'll be right back," our Realtor said, and she left. We kept measuring and after a bit started wondering where she disappeared to. When she came back, she asked us to step outside. Across the street in a cul-de-sac was a house under construction that was almost identical to the house we wanted in the first place. And it was in our price range.

We went to look at it. It was all framed, and the construction crew was just starting to brick the exterior when we walked in. One step over the threshold, and Dave knew it was the house. "This is it," he said. Just as I knew the neighborhood, he knew the place. A feeling of home comes over you, and you just know.

We bought the house. Then the fun began to make it our Dream House. I wanted a screened porch in place of the deck on the back of the house. Alabama gets very buggy in the summer. Why more people did not have screened porches so they could enjoy the outdoors was a mystery to me.

There was a space above the garage meant to be a bonus room. We wanted that studded out too so Dave could finish it to use as his office. Of course, both of those modifications cost extra money, but, hey, this was my dream home. I wanted it to be how I wanted it.

And then I got to have every woman's dream of picking out everything for the interior. I got to pick countertops, cabinets, kitchen appliances, flooring, paint colors, and lighting for the whole house. That was so much fun, even though like most eager homeowners, I did go over the builder's allowance on some extras.

Dave also got some of his wishes granted too. He was able to have the concrete driveway extended and a 30-amp outdoor outlet put in so we could park the travel trailer on the side of the garage. We were in heaven.

Not to be left out, our girls, who were in college in Illinois, picked the paint colors for their rooms. Marissa went with a mauve color, but Alanna picked a bright, neon green for hers. When we checked on the house's progress, we almost panicked when we pulled up and saw a big green splotch on the driveway.

"What did they do to our concrete?" Dave did not sound happy. Then we sheepishly realized it was the green from Alanna's room reflecting through the window onto the newly laid cement. Phew!

I really loved that house. There were some elements I would have changed later, but we never got the chance. After only a year in our dream house, we got orders to move back to Alaska.

Our Second Home Purchase

Under normal circumstances, finding a house can be stressful, but it is even more so when you have only a week to do it. But, believe me, it can be done. In fact, we did it twice, once in Oklahoma and once in Illinois.

When we learned we were moving to Tinker Air Force Base in Oklahoma City, we traveled down from Alaska and had a week to house hunt. Tinker Air Force Base's housing was small, old, and getting ready to be torn down, so the commander authorized Dave to live off base. As the senior chaplain, Dave's position was considered key and essential. Most key and essential officers live on the base to respond quickly if the commander recalls the senior staff for any reason. Command permission was necessary to live off base.

Just as in Alabama, property taxes are low in Oklahoma, making sense to buy rather than rent. I wanted to look in Moore, Oklahoma, a small town about 10 miles southwest of the base. The city had a reputation as a friendly community with lots of amenities nearby. I had the same feeling I did when I found Summerfield in Alabama.

However, our Realtor had other ideas. He wanted to show us houses in Edmond, 22 miles from the base. "All the commanders and colonels live there," he said. But we did not want to be that far from the air force base, and we also did not want a large home for just the two of us. Simply being able to afford a larger house does not mean you should buy it, especially if it does not suit your needs.

We looked at several houses throughout the Oklahoma City area and three or four in Moore before we found "the one." We liked one because it had a large laundry room, but someone else got to it first. When we got to know them, I was glad we got the house we did, which was just across the street. The large laundry room ate into other living spaces that I was happy to have, and the laundry room in the house we bought was fine. The house fit all our criteria, and knowing this was not going to be our forever home, we bought it.

The only worry was Moore's reputation as a "tornado magnet." That reputation was undeserved in my experience. An immense tornado tore up a large swath of the town in 1999. Another one, an F-5 on the Enhanced Fujita Scale, tore through the city in 2013 after we left. But while we lived in Moore, I only remember twice that the sirens went off. So, a tornado magnet? Maybe Moore is just in the wrong place at the wrong times.

Third and Last House

We loved the challenge of buying a house so much we did it again in 2012 when we purchased the home in which we planned to retire. Our son-in-law, Andy, doubted we could buy a house in a week, but we had done it before, so why couldn't we do it again?

This all came about after Dave came home from his deployment in East Africa with an unknown illness that affected his liver. We were preparing to move from Oklahoma to Hawaii. Dave was feeling a bit depressed about his situation and being far from family again. We started to talk about the "when" and "where" of his future retirement. (Ultimately, we moved three more times before it finally happened.)

"I really want to be that pesky grandfather," he said. "Why don't we look for a house in the Bloomington-Normal area. We will be near some grand-children at least."

Marissa and Andy lived in Normal, Illinois. Alanna and Tyler were still in England where Tyler had several more years left in the Air Force, and we knew we could not follow them around the world.

Besides, we liked Normal. It is a lovely midwestern town with all the amenities of a larger locale. With two universities, several colleges, chain-restaurants galore, and quaint downtown areas, Bloomington-Normal fit the bill.

We made a deal with Marissa and Andy. If we bought a house, we would rent it to them at a reasonable rent, and they would take care of it until Dave retired. They could get out of their tiny apartment and have space to hopefully give me grandchildren someday. They agreed, so the hunt was on.

Dave and I decided we wanted a ranch-style home, again. We planned to grow old in this house, and he already had bad knees so avoiding stairs when possible would be a plus. As before, we looked at several options. I was open to a finished basement to give us more living space, and Dave again wanted something with trees. We settled on a four-bedroom, three-bath home in an established area of town. And yes, there were trees, a nature preserve, and a small farm with donkeys right behind the house.

The house had been updated, and the basement was mostly finished with a small family room, a fourth bedroom, and a third full bath. It was also in a friendly, quiet neighborhood. It was perfect. We put in an offer which was accepted, all in one week. Andy and Marissa moved in, got a kitten, got a puppy, and eventually gave us a beautiful little granddaughter.

Lessons Learned:

- *Weigh the pros and cons of living off-base versus on-base. Neither choice is right for every family. Do what is right and makes sense for your family.*

- *Include your spouse equally in a home selection. You might be spending more time there, but this is also the place they will look forward to coming home to.*

CHAPTER 7: PCS NIGHTMARES

We were moving to Hawaii when we bought the Illinois house. Hawaii, right? Paradise. It would be quite a change from Oklahoma. But, wow, Hawaii. Many military friends we knew were dying to get there. And now we would have lived in Alaska twice and Hawaii once. Most people would be happy with either one. People thought we were so lucky. And we were once we got there.

Sure Hope Hawaii Is Paradise Because It's Hell Trying to Get There

We had so much to do to prepare for our move to Hawaii. First, our household goods had to be picked up a few months earlier than usual since it involved overseas travel. We had to find a place to store our travel trailer because it would be of no use on the islands. Then, we had to jump through several hoops just to get our two cats ready to move with us as well.

It is expensive to move animals overseas, and then there is the mandate to quarantine them for 120 days. The animals could be quarantined on the mainland for 120 days, but we did not know we were moving to Hawaii until 90 days before Dave's report date.

I applaud Hawaii for not wanting rabies brought into the islands, but it got to be a little ridiculous. On any move, pets need to have a vet exam and get a certificate showing their vaccinations are up to date. That is routine. But to get the cats into Hawaii, they needed their rabies vaccine AND a titer test to prove the vaccine worked. And then they would go into a state-run quarantine facility at $14 a day, per cat. That plus airfare for the cats was adding up even with some costs being reimbursed. And my big question was, "Why the quarantine if the cats had rabies shot and the titer to show it worked?" Obviously, they did not have rabies.

We could not keep the cats in Illinois where we stayed until Dave had to leave because I was flying from Illinois to England at the end of that May for our first grandchild's birth. So, we could not quarantine them for 120 days before leaving the mainland. Several people told us to give the cats away, but we could not do that. Like many pet owners, they were family and companions. We had raised them from kittens. We got our fluffy gray cat, River, in Alaska when he was three months old. We got Karma, an ill-tempered tabby, from our daughters when they got caught with her in an apartment that did not allow pets. She was a kitten when they rescued her and almost a year old when we took her in. No way were we leaving them behind.

Sadly, a few days before Dave and the cats were to leave, River had a stroke and died in front of us. He was 16 years old. In some ways, that made things a little easier and less expensive, but we were so sad. And guilty because a few days before, I threatened him, saying if he died after we spent all that money for quarantine, I would kill him. So, he died before the trip.

Dave and Karma flew off to Hawaii on May 17, 2012, the day our first grandson, Anthony, made his appearance in the world in England. I had tickets to go to England in two weeks for Tony's birth, but the little guy came three weeks early. Instead of changing to an earlier date, I flew from Illinois two weeks later.

Dave had already found a house for us and had our goods delivered with much of it unpacked by the time I showed up in Hawaii a month later.

When They Destroy Your Stuff

As I have said before, moving is stressful, and you always need to be prepared for some damage to your furniture and other items being lost. On our first move to Alaska, Dave's Trek bicycle and a twin-size box spring went missing. We learned to buy furniture soon after we moved someplace and enjoy it for a few years -- before the movers got a hold of it.

Our stuff had scratches and dings, but we had never had the kind of damage we had on our move from Mississippi to Virginia. I happened to be in Wisconsin for a family reunion. At the same time, Dave stayed behind to receive the shipment of our household goods. Even before we left Mississippi, we knew this would be a tough move, but we ended up with almost $5,000 worth of damage. The last thing you want to do is file a claim because it is tedious and time-consuming. But there was no way we were going to let this slide.

The saga began when the packers came to box up our belongings. The first thing we usually do is show them all the electronics are in working order. Then Dave would pack them in their original boxes. That went fine. The packing went smoothly, we thought, except the foreman had marked all the electronics as "working condition unknown."

A different foreman showed up the next day to finish the packing and loading of the truck. When he gave us the packing slips to sign, we realized we only had half of the papers. The previous foreman forgot to leave his sheets with us.

We also discovered someone else would be driving the truck to Virginia. The second foreman told us our shipment would be taken to the warehouse, unloaded, and then reloaded on another van. Once it got to Virginia, there was a chance it would be emptied into another warehouse and then reloaded again for delivery when we could receive it. Yikes! I just knew with all that handling, some things were going to get broken.

We called the moving company and expressed our concerns. In the meantime, they discovered we had not signed the first set of sheets, so we made a date to meet up and take care of it. During the meeting, they assured me that our goods were not being unloaded from the trailer at their warehouse, and the new driver would just hook up his cab to the trailer.

Dave pointed out that the electronics were marked as "condition unknown" even though he had shown them they all worked. "Oh, that's just to protect the moving company so no one can claim their broken television worked before the move," we were told. I wondered about our protection. What if it did not work once delivered, but the moving company already marked it not working or unknown? In front of them, Dave made a note that he showed all the electronics worked when they picked it up, and the company rep signed under his signature. (It's a good idea to videotape all your electronics working or at least take a photo showing they are on, with a time and date stamp.)

On the day of delivery, I started getting texts from Dave with pictures of damage and breakage. Almost every box had something broken or damaged in some way. The packers put photos on an angle in boxes and then loaded books on top. They jammed homemade items into boxes too small for them, and they ripped the covers off antique books that could not be replaced. It was a nightmare. Probably a good thing I was not there.

Because claim systems are usually complicated, we would not file one on minor damage, but this was different. The claim filing system was online. I spent days filling out what was damaged on each item, how it was damaged, how much it initially cost, and a reasonable estimate to replace it. Some things were priceless. It was maddening.

The moving company finally did send someone to repair some of the furniture at the company's expense, and we received just under $2,000 for the $5,000 we claimed. But this was not just about the money. It was about accountability and fairness.

I had always heard horror stories about moving, but I had never experienced such a move myself. Ironically, this was our 13th military move, our next to last.

Lessons Learned:

- *Remember that a move will involve more than just furniture. You will have to consider everything -- from pets to plants and from china to children!*

- *Realize some moves will be worse than others. Prepare yourself for some damage and determine if it is worth the hassle of filing a claim. If you do file a claim, put every little damaged item on the claim.*

CHAPTER 8: THE FINAL MOVE

Since we knew we wanted to be near family when we retired, moving back to Illinois was an easy decision, and we knew we wanted to live near our daughter, Marissa. So, we decided on central Illinois instead of the state's northern part. This would still put us only a few hours away from my parents in southern Wisconsin and Dave's mom and brother in northern Illinois.

It was a good choice because about a year after Dave retired, his brother Ken had a massive brain bleed. We were close enough to pick up his mom and head to the hospital, where we hung out for several days until Ken was out of the ICU. Also, we were still able to help Ken's wife, Molly, with his care or give her a brief respite whenever needed.

We now live in Normal, Illinois. When friends heard this, they would say, "Vicki and Normal do not go together in the same sentence." Funny, ha-ha.

Normal is the home of Illinois State University. The population is about 52,500. We like it because restaurants, theaters, shopping, a hospital, and family are all close. Its twin city is Bloomington, Illinois, home of Illinois Wesleyan University, with about 76,600 people. Bloomington is also the national headquarters of State Farm Insurance. Most residents of Bloomington-Normal are employed by either State Farm or one of the universities.

Life here is what we hoped for -- quiet, friendly people, close-knit, and a reasonable cost of living.

Moving to Illinois

After we bought the house in 2012, Marissa and Andy moved into it. They paid us a modest rent and acted as property managers for us. It was a good deal for everyone. They got out of their small two-bedroom apartment, and we got someone we trusted to take care of the house for us.

As retirement neared, we had to decide whether we would move into this house, sell it, buy a new home, or renovate. Andy talked about buying it off us, but Marissa was not sure she wanted to stay in it.

We knew we would renovate if we chose to keep it because we found we did not quite like certain features after visiting there several times. After living in military housing for so long, it was important to us to put our own footprint on it.

I was ready for Dave to retire after our stint in Hawaii in 2014, but Dave was not, and then he made colonel, so he owed the military at least three more years. When the kids heard the news, Andy said, "Good, three more years in the house." He did not want the pressure of finding a new home for their family right away.

As luck would have it, by the time we were set to retire, Marissa, Andy, and our granddaughter, Inara, ended up finding a house literally around the corner from ours. It was a little earlier than we all planned, but it was the right house at almost the right time, so they bought it.

This, too, worked out well for all of us. Marissa and Andy closed on their house in October 2017. The previous owners were having some renovations done to their new home and asked if they could stay until their renovations were completed. We would not be moving to Illinois until the following spring. We were using the same contractor as the people Marissa bought her house from, so he would not start on our home renovations until he was done with the first job. It was a little convoluted, but Marissa and Andy moved into their house in late February. Construction on our house started shortly after that.

Renovations

The biggest issue that needed fixing in our new home was the staircase to the basement. It was narrow and steep. The times we visited, I could not imagine carrying laundry up and down those stairs, especially as I aged. They somehow needed to be moved or extended. The first tradesman we interviewed said it could not be done, and he did not want to make any of the changes we wanted anyway. So, we called the second guy, who came out, brainstormed with us, and quoted the job for much less than the first guy estimated. Plus, he did everything we wanted to be done.

We had an extensive renovation to do. In the basement, we wanted to move the stairs, tear down a wall to open the space, move a few other walls, and move the washer and dryer onto the main floor. We also put in a bar and cabinets in the basement. Upstairs we removed a wall and a half-wall to open it up. Oh, and painted the kitchen, dining room, two bedrooms, and the basement, changed out the carpeting in two bedrooms, and tiled areas where walls were moved. Did I mention we also wanted to build a screen porch where the deck was on the back of the house?

It was a big job, and I was surprised how fast the work got done. Still, our contractor did most of the work himself, and he only works on one job at a time, so he can focus entirely on that job.

Just as I did when we built the house in Alabama, I got to pick tile, carpeting, a new light for the dining room, paint colors, and new appliances for the kitchen. I also picked out the built-in bookshelves in the living room and the bar's cabinetry and countertop. It was so much fun.

I almost did not get to do some of that because the day before I was supposed to fly from Virginia to Illinois, Dave came down with a lousy case of influenza. He was quite sick, and I worried about leaving him. But Dave wanted me to go, and I had neighbors check in on Dave frequently. He was down for 11 days! Poor man.

The renovation job started in early March and was finished by May when we were scheduled to move in. After 31 years in the military and 14 moves, we finally had our forever home.

Settling In

After moving in, we unpacked boxes, set up housekeeping, and then left for a five-week trip to the Northeast and Canada before finally coming home and settling in.

We still had lots to do, like hanging pictures, before we could totally settle in, and even two years later, some boxes are not unpacked. But, in the military, the rule is you never unpack the last box because then you will get orders.

One of the most challenging adjustments to make was choosing which grocery store I would go to. I am quite serious. In the military, I shopped at the base commissary. It was an easy choice because we lived on base most of the time. But now we had options, so I spent several weeks in July shopping at various grocery stores to see which one I liked best. I fretted over the decision. Crazy, I know.

I also had to find a hairdresser, dentist, doctor, and veterinarian for Karma. So many things to do.

At the two-year mark in the house, Dave and I began to get a little antsy. Shouldn't we be getting orders? [Shiver.] No, we were not going to move again. We had planned to take a cruise, but then the Coronavirus (COVID-19) hit, and that like many opportunities was canceled. We finally decided to pull our trailer out of storage and go camping at a state park in eastern Illinois near Danville. We also traveled to Delaware to see son-in-law Tyler before he deployed. If I was not relocating, I would at least travel, get away for a while, and have a change of scenery, even if it was only the inside of our trailer and the sunset outside our door.

We are settled in now and finding our way around the community. We are also making new friends and finding favorite restaurants we can give our business to when they are open. I even hung curtains in the living room, only two-and-a-half years after moving in. But hey, what is the hurry? It is not like we are moving again in two years!

Lessons Learned:

- *It's always bittersweet to look for that home where you are going to retire or relocate after service. Don't rush the process, but once you've made the choice, do what you need to do so you can make the house your own.*

- *Reacquaint yourself with the nonmilitary world of grocery stores everywhere and more Starbucks® and Dairy Queens® than you could ever visit in a lifetime!*

PART 3: COMBATING LONELINESS AND THE IMPORTANCE OF FRIENDS

As military spouses, we have all felt isolated from time to time, especially after a PCS. Believe me, it is a normal but unsettling feeling. First, you know no one. You have just moved to a new town (base, post, station), and you have not had time to get your feet wet. You are too busy finding your way around, unpacking boxes, and setting up housekeeping to find your niche. So, you find yourself sitting at home by yourself with no one to talk to.

As a new spouse, you are also beginning a new way of life. Besides the usual adjustment to married life, many other aspects of your life are different, too. The people you have met speak a weird language with talk of TDYs and deployments, the FRG or the A&FRC. Your base may have an OSC and an ESC. Soon your eyes glaze over, and you stop engaging. (See Appendix I for a more complete list of the military's alphabet soup.)

Your first reaction is to run away, back to your hometown where people speak plain English. You can live in your old bedroom with your parents around and go out at night with friends from high school or college, and life will be NORMAL again.

I get it. Any number of military spouses have all been in your shoes. But don't worry, your new routine will develop quickly enough. Here are some ways to help you navigate through this new adventure.

CHAPTER 9:
LEAVING FRIENDS & FAMILY

It is hard when you leave all your friends and family behind. The last base is always your favorite for a while because it is what's most familiar to you. But soon enough, you will get reacclimated and start making new friends.

When you are alone, it is way too easy to get into the trap of relying on social media to be your friend. It is a great tool, but for beating isolation, you face two problems. Number one, you stay too connected to the past. You use it to talk to all your family and friends in your hometown, which is fine, but can they understand what you are going through? Can they advise you on how to get out and make new friends?

Here's the second point to consider. You are less likely to go out into your new world when you can rely on your old pals for socialization. Even worse, it also makes you feel more isolated when you see pictures of your old gang at a party, a bar, or a ballgame without you. Social media is great for staying connected to old friends, like someone you grew up with or friends from a previous base. Just do not use the past to keep you from moving forward and making new friends.

When we moved to our first assignment in Georgia, it was hard on me. I had never lived more than two hours away from my family. All this military stuff was so strange and new. I think I talked to my mom every day for weeks. Those were days before cell phones and Facebook, so a landline became my best friend.

Then I met the neighbor across the street. She had children close to my daughters' age, and I had met some people at the base chapel. But I had not developed my "posse" yet. Between setting up the house and getting the girls ready for their first day of school, I did not have a lot of time to socialize with the neighbors and others during the first few weeks.

Finding Your Posse

Combating loneliness can be more challenging when you live off-base. When we first moved to Tinker Air Force Base in Oklahoma in 2009, we only had one car. We lived nine miles from base, so often, I was home by myself, and I had not really developed a group of friends yet. After about two months of this isolation, Alanna called and said she was worried about me.

"Mom," she said. "You've been there for two months. You don't talk about things you have done with your friends or about any friends at all. Are you okay?"

"Well, honey, I don't get out of the house very often because we only have one car. But don't worry. I'm going out to lunch tomorrow with some new people," I said.

For me, not making friends by that time was unusual since I am not an introvert by nature. I felt the isolation, and it was starting to wear on me. After that lunch, though, my social life picked up tremendously.

You can find your group, posse, clique, whatever you want to call it, in several places. For me, being a chaplain's spouse, the chapel was my go-to place to get the lay of the land. I always knew I could get answers from someone in the chapel.

Your neighbors are always a big help, too, whether you live on base or off. Meet your neighbors. On base, usually, a neighbor or two will stop by to introduce themselves. When we lived in Oklahoma, we baked cookies and were the ones who went to four or five houses introducing ourselves. These neighbors were not military because we were living off base, but don't forget that other military spouses are looking to make friends, too.

Join groups on base, whether it is the spouse club, a Bible study, a sports league, or the squadron spouses' group. You will find people who you will probably mesh with and who have similar interests.

Your spouse's workplace is another place for you to make friends with oth-

51

er couples. You will already have things in common with them.

All you need do is put yourself out there a little bit, and you will find some friends to hang out with. You may not meet your Best Friend Forever in these groups or even at this base, but then again, you just might along the way.

Lessons Learned:

• *Whatever you do, please do not stay isolated. Get out and find your group.*

• *Use social media to post interests and even that you are looking for someone to meet you for coffee or lunch. Others at your base are probably going through the same challenges but don't know how to reach out.*

• *Feeling lonely is the worst feeling in the world, but you do not have to let it overcome you. To find a friend, you only need to be a friend!*

CHAPTER 10: FRIENDS STEP UP

Knowing people and having friends are invaluable for your mental health and sometimes for your physical health. For instance, I broke my foot, and Dave deployed for a month the day after my surgery. Great timing, right?

The Broken Foot

Anyone can break their foot in the winter in Fairbanks, Alaska, but it takes great talent to do it in July. In July 1997, I accepted the challenge. But the experience taught me a great lesson on friendship and how to accept help when it is offered.

There we were on a warm, sunny July morning. I needed to pick up some dry cleaning, so the girls and I hopped into the car and drove to the base dry cleaners. The girls stayed in the car while I walked up the stairs and into the building. As I came out of the cleaners, I remember switching my clothes to my left hand to grasp the railing with my right. The next thing I remember is falling flat on my rear end.

"Are you okay?" asked a worker standing at the top of the stairs, casually smoking a cigarette and talking to some other women. At first, I thought I was, but then I thought twice about trying to stand up. Somewhere in the deep recesses of my mind, I remembered hearing something snap.

"I don't think I am," I said. "I think I broke something. Could you please call my husband at the chapel?" I noticed I still had the dry-cleaning in my hand. One of the other women took it from me and asked if I wanted her to put it in the car. Oh my gosh, the girls are in the car listening to music and probably did not see what happened. "Please, and will you tell my girls to come here?" I asked.

The ambulance arrived, followed by a police car, a fire truck, and the base safety officer. But Dave still was not there. "Did you get a hold of my husband?" The woman said no one answered, so she left a message.

It was odd that no one answered in the middle of the morning at the chapel. Then I realized she probably called the wrong number. She probably used the phone prefix for residents on base, not the prefix for base businesses. She left a message for some poor person that his wife fell and went by ambulance to the clinic. I gave her the correct number, and Dave arrived onsite in a few minutes.

The ambulance drivers, a police officer, and the safety officer all asked me what happened. What happened was that as I descended, a stairstep gave way at the same time as the railing did!

The paramedic removed my shoe to check my foot and ankle. I told him it was my foot and pointed where I felt some discomfort. He pressed all around the spot until he hit the mark, and I said (and I am not lying), "It kind of hurts where you are pressing."

They whisked me to an examining room at the base clinic, followed closely by Dave and the girls. I do not do well in crises without Dave, so I was anxious until my family came into the room. Then shock settled in. I felt light-headed, nauseous, and cool and clammy at the same time. Dave got me some water and asked someone for a blanket.

They asked me to put my right foot flat on the table to get the pictures they needed in radiology. Yeah, that hurt a little. They kept concentrating on the ankle, and I kept saying it was my foot, not the ankle. The x-ray showed my ankle was OK, but a shadow appeared, so they wanted to x-ray the foot. To do this, I re-signed a paper saying I was not pregnant. "Nothing happened in the past 5 minutes," I assured them.

There it was, a long crack in the bones beneath my little toe on my right foot. I broke my fifth metatarsal. Hurray for me!

The paramedics kept coming in to look at the x-ray, not believing I broke my foot. "Most people, when you touch the broken spot, go through the roof. You were like, 'it sort of hurts where you are pressing,'" one of them said.

After looking at the x-ray, Dave made his diagnosis, "You're going to have to have surgery. The break won't heal by itself." Thanks, Mr. Positive.

The emergency room attendants cast my foot and sent me home.

Two days after the accident, late Friday afternoon, the orthopedic surgeon from the Army hospital in Fairbanks called. He asked if the doctor at the clinic set my foot. "No. He put it in a cast and told me I could walk on it this weekend." The doctor chuckled. "You can try." He could tell from the x-ray that the break was more serious. "I need to see you first thing Monday morning."

After trying to manipulate the bones back together, the orthopedic doctor said I needed surgery. Dave was right. Since Dave had a four-week deployment coming up on Friday, we scheduled surgery for Wednesday.

After arriving at the hospital at the crack of dawn, I settled into the bed in the pre-op area, and we waited. And waited. And waited. Finally, at about 1 p.m., Dave asked when my surgery would happen. The nurses seemed shocked I was still there. Then they panicked because the surgery staff had gone to lunch. Speaking of lunch, I had not eaten since dinner the night before. I was starving. It turned out the team had not gone to lunch. The delay was due to my meticulous doctor who ran late during the previous surgery.

I opted for spinal anesthesia with the twilight drugs so I would not hear anything during the surgery. I imagined hearing the doctor call for a drill or a hammer and chisel. I did not want to know. I do remember one part of the surgery. I heard the doctor ask how long he had left. A nurse answered it had been 90 minutes already, and then someone tapped my hand as I tried to take the tourniquet off my thigh.

I awoke in a ward with other patients. The doctor, expressing concern over the pain I might experience as the anesthetic wore off, admitted me for the night. Dave was anxious about that. I had to get out on Thursday because of his upcoming trip.

I begged Dave to stay home, but a spouse in a non-weight bearing cast for eight weeks is not a reason to postpone a deployment. I worried about eating macaroni and cheese for the next four weeks because that was the only meal my 12-year-old girls knew how to cook.

But help came in the form of neighbors, chapel friends, and the spouses of the squadron members who deployed with Dave. I am not a person who can ask for aid easily. I like to think I am the strong, independent military spouse I am supposed to be. This experience was humbling. I could not drive, could barely walk, and had to care for my two preteen children. These friends really stepped up.

One friend, Nancy, cleaned my house. Cathie drove me to my doctor's appointments 30 miles away with her two small children in tow, and a third friend coordinated meals for us for four weeks. Cathie even kept me supplied with Twizzlers® and cleaned out the refrigerator when I could smell something horrible. Nancy had the dubious pleasure of helping me shower. Anything I needed to be done, they made it happen. This incident taught me what it means to be part of the Air Force family and how much people really care for each other. You just have to ask.

Since then, I have received help and given help when I can to my military friends, neighbors and even a few strangers. Because as all military spouses know, nothing goes wrong until your spouse deploys.

Another Time Friends Rescued Me

Another time that friends came to the rescue was when I had a kidney stone. It was a Friday, of course. Nothing serious happens during the week, only on Fridays or the weekend when the medical facility is closed. And, of course, Dave was deployed to the Middle East at the time.

Anyway, there I was, watching my friend's toddler, Kimberly, when I felt a sharp twinge in my back radiating to the front. I had had kidney stones before, and I recognized the pain. I vomit when I have that kind of pain, so I grabbed the baby and headed for the bathroom.

As I lay on the bathroom floor with the baby next to me, I thought of my options. I knew I needed to go to the doctor, but what could I do with Kimi? As soon as the pain subsided and I stopped vomiting, I made my way to the phone in the kitchen. (Again, this was before we had cell phones.) I tried to call Kimi's mom but I could not reach her. Great. Now, what do I do?

The first problem was finding someone who could watch Kimi. My friend Shelly might do it if she were not busy. I called her, and she came right over. The second problem was I needed to get to the doctor, but I was in too much pain to drive myself. I thought of another friend, Laurie. Her husband was a commander at the hospital. Maybe she could take me. Thankfully, Laurie was free and immediately offered to drive me. I could not get an appointment with my doctor, but I could be seen by the medical team as a walk-in. Our medical care was broken up into caregivers' sections, so if you did not see your primary doctor, a team member could take you. They had access to all your records.

The receptionist sent me to the waiting room, and a nurse came in to talk to me. After hearing my symptoms, she requested a urine sample. I waited some more, and then the results came back -- I had a kidney stone. The nurse said to go home and get some rest and take Tylenol® for the pain. That did not sound right to me because I was on some heavy painkillers the first time I had a kidney stone. But I did what they said.

Laurie drove me home, Kimi's mother came and picked her up, and everyone left me alone. Laurie told me to call her if I thought I needed more potent pain relief, and she would call her husband. Later in the day, I did, and her husband wrote me a prescription and he brought the medication to me.

I emailed Dave that I had another kidney stone, and he was deeply concerned. He said he remembered how much pain I was in with the first one. I assured him that our friends were taking good care of me and not to worry.

Somewhere along the line that weekend, I passed the stone and felt much better.

In retrospect, he really could not have done anything else for me if he were home that our friends had not done for me. I was so thankful for friends who stepped up to help in a crisis.

Lessons Learned:

• *New friends are great, but try to keep in touch with those people you met at previous bases. It's comforting that they know your history, while your new friends will help you to move forward.*

• *The military truly is a family. Don't be afraid to ask for help. And make sure you help out others in their time of need. You are not alone.*

CHAPTER 11: WHEN FRIENDS DIE

Sometimes in the military, the unthinkable happens, and someone you know dies. It is a horrible experience. We mourn whenever we hear that a plane went down or someone was killed in battle, but it is much worse when it is someone you know. Unfortunately, that happened to us more than once. One was a plane crash, one was a friend's son who was killed in battle, and one was a senseless killing in Afghanistan.

Death of a Friend

My neighbor called me one afternoon in April of 1995, just three years after Dave had joined the service. "I have to tell you something. Can you come over?" I knew right away something was wrong. I told the girls I was going to Sandy's and ran across the street, where she was sitting on her front porch. "Brian Freemont died yesterday," Sandy said. I grabbed the nearest chair and plopped into it before my knees buckled. "Oh, poor Margie," That was the first thought that came into my mind. "What happened?"

The Freemonts were our neighbors for two years. They moved to Virginia in 1994, where Brian had a job at the Pentagon. Margie and Sandy were best friends in Georgia. They were looking forward to being together again when Sandy's family also moved to northern Virginia. Margie heard about the plane crash on the news because the assistant secretary of the Air Force was onboard. She knew it was Brian's plane and called a friend in Virginia who then called Sandy. "I've been on the phone all night with Margie," Sandy said. It would be several more days before Margie got the official news.

Our community was stunned. Brian and Margie were both well-known and respected. They were active on base, in the local town, their church, and the lives of their three sons. I did not know what to do or say. Sandy was our go-between, passing messages to and from Margie and keeping us all in the loop about arrangements for his funeral.

As a minister's wife, I had been around death before, but this was the first active-duty death of a friend. I felt incredibly vulnerable. This could happen to any one of us anytime. I thought of all the things Dave did for the girls and me like helping around the house, playing with the girls, putting them to bed, and always making sure we were his priority. I could not imagine picking up that slack for the rest of my life. I vowed I would never let him leave the house without telling him I loved him—the same for the girls. Today, after all these years, we always say "I love you," whether on the phone, video chat, or text.

This incident so early in our military career taught me the importance of rallying together with friends in times of need and having each other's back. You never know when you will be needed or might need someone supporting you.

Every Death Seems Senseless

Brian Freemont's death hit me harder than it did Dave. I knew Margie better, and I easily pictured myself in her shoes if anything ever happened to Dave. But when David Brodeur died in Afghanistan, it really hit my husband hard, and because he was deployed at the time, I couldn't even hug him. All I could do was listen when he needed to talk.

The Brodeurs lived across the street from us at Eielson Air Force Base in Alaska during our second assignment there. Klepto, which was his call sign, died on April 27, 2011, at the hand of an Afghani soldier gone rogue.

At the time, my Dave was deployed to Camp Lemonnier, Djibouti, the Horn of Africa, and I was in Oklahoma. Dave recorded his feelings in the journal he was keeping during his deployment: April 27, 2011 – "Biggest news tonight – a friend just wrote me that David "Klepto" Brodeur died in Afghanistan today. Dave and Susie lived across the street from us on Misty Fjord at Eielson."

Klepto and Dave served together in the 354th Fighter Wing at Eielson

Air Force Base, Alaska. Dave was the unit chaplain for the 18th Aggressor Squadron, the "Blue Foxes."

The journal entry continued: "Klepto was a man of great faith, a wonderful father. He had a kind word and a great smile. More than just his family will miss him. Pray for his family, his friends, his squadron, and those who died with him."

A veteran Afghan air force pilot opened fire in a meeting room, killing Klepto and eight others during a daily meeting with Afghan officers. An Afghan soldier also died in the attack. According to an Afghan Defense Ministry statement, "The pilot opened fire on foreigners after an argument during the meeting."

The Americans carried sidearms by NATO regulations, so we do not understand how the pilot could kill all 10 people. The assassin died of gunshot wounds in a different part of the building, according to media reports.

Klepto's death serves as a reminder of how dangerous the military can be for those who protect us and our allies.

"The sense of loss always hits hard," Dave wrote. "I have met some callous people who said, 'Well, you chose this life. I don't feel sorry for you.' Many folks don't understand the calling of service or understand if good people don't offer their health, their limbs, or even their life; plenty of bad guys would love to take the blessings of this land and its people and change them to something else," Dave noted in his journal.

"Klepto was one of those who said, 'Here I am, send me.' I can only imagine what his last day on Earth was like. We in the Air Force expect to lose some people in aircraft incidents, not executed by an Afghan going postal."

On May 10, 2011, Dave led a memorial service for the nine American soldiers who were killed. About 80 people attended the voluntary service, including the Camp Lemonnier Commander, unit commanders, and representatives from all the service branches at Camp Lemonnier. Volunteers from each service branch read a short biography of the victims. Camp Lemonnier Public Affairs also filmed the service and sent a copy to each of the fallen families.

Dave took comfort in knowing that Klepto was a faithful Christian man, husband, father, son, friend, and wingman.

"He did not die alone, and the world is a better place because of his life. I know God has a special place just for him," he wrote.

We've known others who have died, and it never gets any easier. Two close friends died at their own hand, while a third was the son of neighbors at Eielson, who was killed in Iraq. Sometimes your first thought is thankfulness that it wasn't your spouse or child. But then the reality hits, and your heart goes out to those who lost their loved ones.

We can't do much to ease the pain the family or our own spouse is experiencing. We can only hold them as they sob and listen to them as they try to process what they feel.

Lessons Learned:

- *The reality is bad things do happen. All you can do is be present for each other, listen, and support each other through the tough times.*

- *Be aware that your spouse may experience grief and loss differently than you do.*

- *When someone is grieving, silence is not golden. Maybe your spouse doesn't want to talk about it with you. If so, encourage your loved one to seek out the professionals who can help them to heal. Chaplains and mental health counselors are always available.*

CHAPTER 12: FOREVER FRIENDS

Occasionally, you meet someone who you know is your kindred spirit, as Anne Shirley said in the book Anne of Green Gables. I have four such like-minded souls in my life.

I met Linda before Dave joined the military. She has twin daughters a week older than mine. The four girls were two years old when we met. Her birthday is the day after mine, although she is five years older, something I never let her forget. We bonded over the twin thing and have been fast friends ever since. She is someone I can always call on for help or just a good laugh.

I met Mary in Alabama at our church off base. She was pulling my husband's pant leg up to see his socks (really, that's how we met!). She is also older than me, and after being the oldest member of my posse too many times, it was nice to hang out with someone more senior for a change. She, also, is someone I can call on whenever the need arises.

Then there is Kraig, my BFF (Best Friend Forever). We met on our way from Alaska to Oklahoma while driving through Colorado. He was going to be a chaplain on Dave's staff at Tinker Air Force Base in Oklahoma City. He was stationed in Wyoming and agreed to meet us in Colorado for breakfast. I liked him right away. Kraig ended up helping us change a tire on our trailer before going our separate ways. In Oklahoma, we became good friends. I initially called him my "boy" friend, but he was uncomfortable with that, so I changed it to my BFF.

And then, in Alaska in 2006, Dave and I met Marlene and David, who lived at the end of our cul-de-sac, and they became our best military-couple friends. Although both men are retired from the Air Force now, we keep in touch frequently, travel to see each other, and even took a cruise together.

Military Friends Become Family

As I said, whenever we move, we must make new friends. Although we knew some people, we still needed to find our crowd, our posse, whatever you want to call it. We made most of our friends on our block or at the officers' club.

One of my first friends in Alaska the second time was Marlene. She and I met when we went on a tour of the base for new commanders' spouses. Her husband, David, was deployed when we moved in. Later that week, she gave my Dave a ride home, and a few weeks later, at an Officers' Spouse Club meeting, she asked to sit with me. That was the start of a lifelong friendship. You know how you have friends, but only a few who are FRIENDS? Marlene became one of those for me. Her husband filled the same void for my husband when he returned home from his deployment.

Soon our families were inseparable. If I went somewhere without Marlene, people asked me where she was. For Dave and me, being so far away from our daughters, who were in college in Illinois, Marlene and David's daughter, Sarah, became our surrogate child. We watched her grow from a gangly teenager into a beautiful young woman. When Sarah was commissioned as a second lieutenant in the U.S. Air Force in 2014, she used Dave's old second lieutenant bars to pin on her uniform. Passing on your former rank insignia to someone who was just promoted to that rank is a special honor and an Air Force tradition. The following weekend, Dave performed the marriage ceremony for Sarah and her high school sweetheart, Jake.

We did not get to know their other daughter, Jennifer, because she was away at boarding school and then college. Still, we do see her at family gatherings and get to watch her family grow and blossom too.

I remember celebrating our first Thanksgiving together. Marlene loved to play hostess, so each year, the meal was at their house. I am sure I brought a dish to add to the abundance of food, but I do not remember exactly what they were. When I wanted to take some leftovers home, Marlene refused to give me any. I did not know what to think about that the first time. But her rule was if we wanted leftovers, we had to come back to their house for dinner. So, for the next three nights after Thanksgiving, we ate dinner at their home.

Since we met in 2006, David and Marlene are part of our family. We have supported them through adopting a little boy who has special needs. We have rejoiced over promotions, the birth of grandchildren, and now retirement. We even went on a cruise together to celebrate their 25th wedding anniversary. David and Dave frequently talk to keep up with the happenings in each other's lives, and we look forward to sharing more life experiences.

Lessons Learned:

• *Close friends will pop-up when you least expect it. Nurture the relationship so it becomes a lifelong friendship.*

• *Some friends enter your life for a season, but others are in it for the long haul.*

PART 4: DEPLOYMENTS

Deployments are different than temporary duty assignments, although technically, they are temporary duty assignments because the orders do not call for a permanent change of station, or PCS. As Dave explained it, a deployment supports a named mission, like Desert Shield/Desert Storm or Operation Deny Flight. It usually is on foreign soil.

Dave was deployed eight times during his years in the Air Force. For some, that is not many. Army, Navy, and Marines deploy far more frequently and for much longer. Dave's longest deployment was about eight months. Acknowledging that others deploy for a year or more makes me more empathetic, but it does not make the separation easier. And just like Murphy's Law, deployment rules still apply -- if something is going to go wrong, and it will, it invariably happens while your spouse is deployed.

Pre-Deployment

Deployments come in three phases. First, there is the pre-deployment time. This is when your spouse comes home and announces they are going to deploy. The announcement usually comes months in advance, but it could come within days or even hours of deployment. Even knowing weeks in advance is no guarantee that the date won't get changed – several times.

Pre-deployment is the time to get ready before your spouse actually leaves. This usually means that as they get all their deployment gear ready, you have uniforms, gas masks, and a pile of supplies scattered all over your living room.

The two of you need to have the hard talk about what if something happens, not an easy subject to discuss but absolutely necessary. You should take this time to go over finances, wills, powers-of-attorney, and where to find all these essential papers.

Let me give you some advice on powers-of-attorney. You should definitely have a general power-of-attorney, but recognize that it does not do much good. I could buy a house or a car with Dave's general power-of-attorney. Still, I could not use it to deposit a check from our insurance company into our joint savings account. I also could not get any financial information about his pay with it. There are special powers-of-attorney for all those situations. Ask the base lawyer which ones you need. At no cost to you, the base lawyer's office can draw up a will and all the powers-of-attorney you need before your spouse leaves.

Pre-deployment is also the time to make memories with your family. When times get tough, you can remember how much fun you had and how much fun you will have again when your spouse returns home.

But, if you are like me, you might find yourself beginning to draw away from your spouse. I never did it consciously, but Dave once pointed out to me that I was pushing him away just when he wanted us to be closer. It was my safety mechanism against hurting too much when he left. In my mind, I thought if I started doing things on my own before he deployed, maybe it wouldn't be too bad when he actually left. Try not to do this. Enough changes are coming. Always enjoy your time together whenever you can.

Phase 2 is the deployment itself. Read on.

CHAPTER 13: WORRYING AND OTHER TRAVAILS OF DEPLOYMENTS

While we lived in Hawaii, Dave traveled to Asia quite a bit. One trip co-incided with North Korea leader Kim Jong-un announcing he had nuclear missiles and planned to launch one against Hawaii. People who knew where Dave was asked me if I was nervous about his safety given the North Korean announcement. I laughed. I figured Dave was safer in Asia than I was in Hawaii since we were the named target.

Seriously though, I think we all worry about our spouses while they are gone. Anything can happen at any time. As a chaplain, Dave is a non-combatant. It is against the Geneva Convention of 1949 for chaplains to handle a weapon while in a deployed zone. He had to rely on his chaplain assistant, who was a combatant, to provide protection if necessary. For a quick second I did worry after learning his assistant was a 5-foot, 100-pound female! But really, no matter their size or gender, these assistants were highly trained in the use of the weaponry.

I did come up with one rule that gave me some comfort: Dave could not tell me about any of the crazy things that happened during his deployment until he was standing in front of me and I could see he was safe and sound. That rule came about when he was still in the reserves in the late 1980s. He worked with a C-130 flying unit, and they were in Denver to pick up some nurses to give them a lift back to Pennsylvania. This is Dave's version of what happened as he described AFTER he returned home safely. For me, ignorance was bliss.

"I was on board a C-130, flying for over an hour in the middle of, and around severe thunderstorms, around Denver/Colorado Springs.

"I don't normally get anxious flying unless the aircrew gets anxious. Our navigator was an FAA air controller when he was not flying with the Air Reserve. He looked at me at one point and said, 'Chaplain, we really need your prayers. They keep vectoring us into the thunderheads!' As you can guess, it was like riding a bucking bronco for over an hour."

Dave continued recounting the scary details. "We had to pick up a bunch of medical folks and fly them to Pittsburgh. When we were finally allowed to land, we were the only aircraft moving as the runway, taxiway, and ramp had about 10 inches of hailstones. We had a short window to load folks and take off before the next round of storms. Also, the power was knocked out in the whole area, including the air terminal.

"We did a 'hot-on-load,' meaning the engines were still running while we piled the folks and their gear into the back. As the medics got on board, many of them rubbed my head for good luck [kind of like how folks would rub Buddha's stomach for good luck] and said they were glad I was aboard.

"Our Loadmasters strapped everything down and our people in, passed out airsickness bags, and we did about as close to a vertical take-off as a C-130 can do. Thanks be to God, we literally snuck out between two massive thunderheads, and, obviously, I'm still here today."

All I knew was they were late getting home, and I had not heard from Dave. Then the phone rang.

"Hello?"

"Mrs. Terrinoni?" a voice said on the other end of the line.

"Yes."

"This is Colonel ..."

That's all I heard. My heart leaped into my throat. I didn't even catch her name.

"I just wanted to let you know that your husband just took off from Pittsburgh after dropping us off. He is fine and should be home shortly," she said.

I thanked her and hung up the phone, sighing with relief. In my head, I knew if something happened to Dave, a blue car with two or three people in uniform would come to the house, knock on the door, and give me the bad news. My heart did not listen to reason when the telephone rang, and I was scared for a minute or two.

Even though Dave was in some dangerous places, he was never in a firefight, though he has been close. When he was in Africa, his camp was 10 miles from Somalia. Some of his trips took him to an area of Kenya where Somalian pirates were kidnapping people. On one Skype call, he suddenly ducked out of the picture and said he heard gunshots. (Thanks for that knowledge, dear.) Luckily the shooting was not near him.

In another instance, the week he left his classified site in Bahrain to come home, the base went to Force Protection Delta. Force Protection Delta is the highest level of preparedness for an attack. Military members don their protective gear, or "battle rattle," and stay in bunkers until the all-clear sounds. I heard it on the news, so when I met him at the airport, I said, "So, you were in Delta this week, huh?"

His assistant smacked him in the arm and said, "You told her?"

"Relax," I replied. "It was on the news."

Speaking of the news, when your spouse is deployed to a combat zone, it is best not to watch the news too much. I had a friend in Georgia who stayed glued to CNN during Desert Shield/Desert Storm. Her husband was flying with Gen. Norman Schwarzkopf, who was the commander of United States Central Command at the time. My friend often knew where her husband was because she could see him standing behind or beside the general in news videos.

It was good to know where her husband was and that he was safe at that moment, but not when she could also see Scud missiles soaring through the sky or bombs bursting nearby. She was a basket case by the time he got home.

Some knowledge is okay, but sometimes it is too much.

The Checkbook Story

I learned how much Dave did around the house the first time he deployed, and I had to absorb his duties as well as my own. We tend to take for granted having our spouse around to take out the garbage, mow the lawn, help with housework, or pay the bills until we must tackle them ourselves.

I had the responsibility of handling the bills off and on throughout our 10-year marriage, and I knew how to balance a checkbook and such. Still, for some reason, when Dave deployed to France for one week in 1994, I fell apart over my unbalanced checkbook. It was not even off by that much, but for the life of me, I could not get that sucker to balance.

Suddenly, it threw me into a tizzy. I started crying, then screaming. I do not remember for sure, but I probably threw the checkbook across the room. I checked and re-checked all the canceled checks against the bank statement. I went back and checked all the figures through the whole registry, and still, I could not find the error.

This scared me because if I were so upset over something so minor, what would happen when Dave left for a long time? How on earth would I handle a more prolonged deployment if I could not even bear one week?

Of course, the checkbook was not the main reason I was so upset. I was more upset about my inability to handle situations or challenges on my own. I questioned whether this whole military thing was going to work. On top of all that, it did not help that Dave was in France, a place I wanted to go some time.

One night he called and said, "I just had the best crepes I've ever had."

His comment was met with a moment of stony silence until I answered, "Oh yeah? Well, we had hot dogs and macaroni and cheese." That was his lesson for the future to gauge what kind of mood I was in before he commented on his meals.

Since then, we have what we call a t-shirt deployment or a better-than-a-t-shirt deployment. Depending on where Dave goes and how badly I want to see that locale determined if he could get away with bringing me just a t-shirt or if my gift must be something better than a t-shirt.

As for the checkbook, I finally took it over to my neighbor for a fresh set of eyes. She found the mistake quickly and assured me I would handle the next deployment just fine.

Just Slap Me and Tell Me to Buck Up

I handled most of his other deployments fairly well. In fact, I got to visit him in Italy on one of his deployments, so that was a bonus. But there was one separation that really got to me while we lived in Alaska in 1997.

This deployment had several strikes against it. First, he would be deployed for four months. We had never been separated that long. Second, it was over the Christmas holiday. We had never been apart over the holidays. And third, it was winter in Fairbanks, Alaska, when the sun rises just over the mountains for maybe three hours before sinking below the horizon again. I was miserable, but I tried not to show it.

It all started the Sunday before Dave left. Everyone was praying for Dave's safe travels in the chapel and a safe deployment for Dave, and Dave this and Dave that. What about me? I left the sanctuary and hid out in his office for the rest of the service. I was throwing myself one good pity party, and it was not going to be the last one I threw during that deployment.

I felt no one was taking my loneliness and my feelings into consideration. I mean, I was going to be alone at Christmas with our two preteen daughters. We could not afford to go home to Chicago for the holidays. Before the holiday arrived, I waited for someone to invite us over for dinner, but the invitation never came. I tried to make things as traditional as possible for the girls, but it was hard without Daddy home. And then on Christmas Day, I thought about him, all alone in his room, opening his presents by himself, and I felt lucky to have the girls with me.

We were fortunate on this deployment. On previous deployments, Dave got one phone call a week for 15 minutes, and emails were not generally used. But this time, because we lived in a remote location, we got morale calls. He got four a week, and I got three. They were only for 15 minutes, but still, we got to talk for 15 minutes a day! I split the time with each of the girls, so we each got five minutes for six days. That is not a lot of time to spend complaining or moaning about how lonely you are, so I did not. Fridays were our "date" night, and I got the whole 15 minutes! The operator, who placed our calls, knew that it was date night and actually would be excited for us!

Frequently during this deployment, I cried myself to sleep. I cannot even point out what was so bad or challenging about it; it just was. All the books I read on surviving deployments said not to share your hard times with your spouse. The military member needed to focus on their mission and did not need to be worried about what was happening at home. Only good news was to be shared.

But one date night, I could not take it any longer, and I told him how I was feeling. This guy is my best friend. I should share my feelings with my best friend, shouldn't I? I remembered how he told me about times when he had to counsel a spouse who wanted him to sign an early-return-of-dependent form allowing the family to move back to the Lower 48 before the military member. Not all people are cut out to spend three years in Alaska. I used to tell Dave to "slap those spouses and tell them to buck up." Through my tears on that date night, I told him I needed him to "slap me and tell me to buck up."

Pouring my feelings out helped somewhat, but I was still having a hard time. Dave even offered to get out of the military if I wanted him to, but how could I demand that of him? I knew I would survive the deployment. The military and chaplaincy were his callings, and I could not ask him to give it up. He loved it too much, and I loved him too much.

Then one day, I had to deliver something to a colonel's wife. She asked me how I was doing, and it all came pouring out. I had been trying to put on a happy facade all this time, not letting anyone know I was not coping. But you know what? She knew what I was going through. She had been there herself. After that talk, I felt much better. I did not feel so alone, and I knew I would be able to hang on until Dave came home.

However, I talked him into letting the girls and me go to Illinois for spring break to boost our morale. I threatened to go to Anchorage for a weekend and get tattoos if we didn't go to Illinois. We had a wonderful trip to the Land of Lincoln.

Where You Go, I Will Go

Lessons Learned:

• *You are not alone during a deployment. Other spouses have been through the same things. Tell someone what you are feeling and let them help you.*

• *It's okay to throw a pity party, but don't let it last too long. Do what you have to do to live your life during the deployment.*

CHAPTER 14: AFRICA

In November 2010, Dave left for a seven-month deployment to East Africa. He served as the Deputy Command Chaplain and Deputy Director of Religious Affairs for The Combined Joint Task Force-Horn of Africa stationed in Djibouti. But his job took him all over East Africa. He worked with Civil Affairs Teams to build relationships with local religious and community leaders to keep radical factions out of these areas. His job took him to Ethiopia, Uganda, Kenya, Tanzania, and the Comoros Islands, and he worked with locals in Djibouti.

The day he left, I threw a pity party. After my first pity party in Alaska, I learned it was okay to have one day to feel sorry for yourself and then get on with your life. When the girls were home, we would have a chick-flick night and sleep in the living room. My pity party looked more like me devouring a bag of Twizzlers® while watching chick-flicks. Only I did it with the two cats instead of my two girls. After that, I spent my time volunteering, socializing, and visiting Marissa and Andy in Illinois and my parents in Wisconsin.

It turned out to be his longest and last deployment. It was also the first one I went through on my own since both girls were married and out of the house. Dave frequently referred to it as his financial recovery deployment after paying for two weddings that summer. My expenses were cut in half without feeding him, which helped build our savings back up.

First Deployment on My Own

I was worried about being alone for seven months when Dave deployed to East Africa. Previously, I had the girls with me. But they were both married and had lives of their own. Marissa and Andy lived in Illinois, and Alanna and Tyler were in Alaska. Tyler was also deployed to the Middle East about a month after Dave left, so Alanna was alone. But she had a job to keep her busy and get her out of bed in the morning. I had none of that.

Ultimately, it turned out to be one of our best deployments. Not only was Dave's mission incredible, but I learned how to be on my own. It was so freeing to be able to eat what I wanted when I wanted. I could go to the movies by myself and see what I wanted to see. Everything was on my timetable. I did not have to see if Dave's schedule lined up with what I wanted to do.

Also, I volunteered at the base thrift shop, which kept me busy, and I continued to participate in all the groups I belonged to through the Officers' Spouse Club. Sometimes I got bored, but I really relished my time at home by myself.

Of course, I missed Dave. I had to go to some base functions like the National Prayer Luncheon alone. Still, another chaplain was single, and he escorted me to several events, too, or we went as a chapel group.

We were far enough along in Dave's career and had been at our base long enough that I had my own circle of friends, and I was not afraid to ask for help. I knew several people who were always happy to help if needed—all part of being in the military family.

Having to Tell Him to Stop Calling So Much

What made this deployment okay was the communication we shared. It changed so much from Dave's first deployment in 1994 until this last one in 2010. Skype® was a significant improvement. Once, Dave Skyped with me in Oklahoma, Marissa in Illinois, and Alanna in Alaska all at the same time-- while he was in the middle of Ethiopia. We were able to talk and see each other almost every day. In fact, Dave had a Saturday off once, and he Skyped me three times. I finally had to tell him that I had things I needed to do and could not stay glued to the computer all day. That is a far cry from the days I would hang by the phone waiting for his short, weekly 15-minute call.

Since he was deployed and traveled to small villages, sometimes Dave would be unavailable to talk. He would tell me when this might happen and always let me know when he was back in Internet range so I would not freak out when I could not reach him.

Email was also an excellent way to stay in touch. We wrote to each other every day. He later told me he missed receiving actual letters from me. I have never been a good letter writer, but I kept it in mind after that.

Traveling Solo

I also learned to travel by myself. If I did not want to be alone for Christmas, I would have to make the drive to Illinois by myself. It was about a 14-hour drive, and I made that trip a couple times while Dave was gone. I also went to my parents in Wisconsin a few times.

For Easter 2011, I planned to leave for the 14-hour drive to Illinois on Good Friday. The weather forecast called for bad storms in Missouri and Illinois that day, so I decided to go on Thursday instead. Someone forgot to tell the storms to wait until Friday. It was raining in Oklahoma when I left, but it wasn't too bad. Driving was slower because of the rain and high winds, so it took me a lot longer. The storms really blew up just as I was reaching the outskirts of St. Louis, but I really couldn't do anything but keep going. Later, I heard a tornado was spotted at the St. Louis Airport about the time I passed it. When I finally made it to Marissa and Andy's house, they were in bed and had to get up to let me in.

While I was in Illinois, I called my parents to wish them a Happy Easter, and I learned my mom was in the hospital with bronchitis. She was coming home the next day, so I extended my trip for a week to help her. If Dave were with me, I could not have done that because he would have had to go back to work. Sometimes things work out for the best.

Meet Up in Paris

During Dave's East Africa deployment, he was scheduled to go to a conference in Vicenza, Italy, for a week. Did I want to meet him there? Have

I mentioned that Italy is my favorite European country? I had never been to Vicenza, a city in northeastern Italy not far from Venice, so that would be a new experience.

We arranged our flights to meet up in Paris, fly to Venice, and then drive to Vicenza together. I was happy to be able to see Dave in the middle of his deployment.

We flew to Venice and discovered my luggage was still in Paris. Here I am in another country with no clean underwear. The hotel we stayed at was in a posh section of Vicenza, and while there were several haute-couture designer shops, they were not stocked with clothes for the "mature woman." I ended up having to wear the same clothes the next day until my luggage was located and delivered to our room. Great impression to make on people you have never met before, but everyone understood.

I learned an essential lesson that trip -- always pack an extra day's underclothes in your carry-on.

The rest of the trip was terrific. While the military members were in meetings, the spouses gathered for day trips. My favorite was the pottery factory, where dishes are made for Lenox® and several other china companies. I picked up a set of Italian pottery dishes and several smaller items for family gifts. It was so much fun. Dave and I also did some shopping around the hotel. The tanzanite stone he bought for me when he was in Tanzania we had set into a beautiful necklace. I like these trips where I get to spend money. Obviously, this was a better-than-a-t-shirt deployment.

Soon, the conference was over, and we had to go our separate ways. But it was a once-in-a-lifetime event that lives fondly in our memories. However, it would not be the only time I flew through Paris to get to Venice, and they lost my luggage then, too. But that's another story for another time. I will try hard not to fly to Venice via Paris again.

The Tornado

Dave would be home near the end of May 2011, and I was starting to get excited. But I had one more thing I had to do before he got home. I had to survive an Oklahoma tornado. In a previous chapter, I talked about how Moore, Oklahoma, was called a tornado magnet. But we only had two times the sirens went off while we lived there -- May of 2010 and May of 2011.

The local television station programming was interrupted because of massive storms and tornadoes moving through the area. Usually, I am annoyed by this because I could not watch my shows. But that day in 2011 was different. An outbreak of tornados was reported throughout parts of central Oklahoma and had already caused damage and some injuries. I never saw the colors on the weather map include a black spot before, but this one did. I also never heard the weatherman say we needed to be in an underground shelter because the bathroom or closet would not protect us. We did not have an underground shelter in our garage, as many others did.

I started making plans for what I would do. I packed a backpack with my medicines, some other needed items, tried to figure out where I would go and how soon I needed to leave. I briefly thought about putting the cats in their carriers but decided they would be better off loose to hide under something if they needed to.

The neighbor across the street did not know of any shelters in town. All I knew was the neighbor next door had a shelter in their garage. So, I called.

"This is Vicki," was all I said.

"Come on over," my neighbor answered immediately.

"I will when the siren goes off." In less than 15 minutes, the sirens went off, and I joined my neighbor and her three daughters in their shelter.

All Dave knew on his end from the base in Djibouti was that a large tornado was barreling its way toward Moore, and he was on another continent.

While in the shelter, my neighbor kept trying to reach her husband, who was stuck at work in Oklahoma City. In the meantime, Marissa heard about the storm and called my cell phone. I assured her I was safe in the shelter. Since she was tracking the storm on the Weather Channel, I asked her to keep us updated. We had no way of knowing when the warning would be lifted because we could not hear the siren in the shelter, and my neighbor still could not reach her husband on his cell phone. About 30 minutes later, Marissa called to say we were in the clear. I was amused that my daughter in Illinois had to let me know I could get out of a shelter in Oklahoma.

Several tornados including an EF-5, considered the most destructive, touched down throughout the area, destroying homes, businesses, trees, and powerlines. Sadly, 11 people died and nearly 300 others were injured by the massive storms. This was one of the few times that the spouse was potentially in harm's way rather than the military member.

Return to Me in the Same Condition!

It seemed that anytime Dave deployed, he came home sick or broken, and this ticked me off. I sent him away perfectly healthy, but I never got him back in the same condition. When you lend someone something, you expect to get it back in the same state, or maybe even better. Am I wrong?

Once, he came home with salmonella. Another time he came home on crutches. He also came home with an upper respiratory infection and a sinus infection. But when he came home from East Africa, he brought home an unknown disease that was not diagnosed for several years.

All we knew was his liver enzymes were sky high, and a nurse insisted he had to stop drinking immediately. He had not had any alcohol since before he went to East Africa. I talk more about Dave's illness in Chapter 17. Let it suffice to say none of our local doctors seemed to pick up on the fact that he just returned to the United States after seven months in East Africa.

Post Deployment

The third phase of deployment is post-deployment. This is the reunion phase, and for many families, this is the hardest part of a deployment. Things have changed. You've changed. Your spouse has changed, and your children have definitely changed, both physically and emotionally, since before the deployment.

I remember when Dave was deployed in 1998, he came home, and his post-pubescent daughter had developed breasts. He looked at her, did a double-take, and said, "Where did those come from?" When he left, she was a little girl, but now she was blossoming into a young lady. I don't think he was ready for that.

The best post-deployment advice I ever received was to treat the returning spouse as a guest for a few days. Let them observe changes and differences in how the household is run before having them pitch in again. Sometimes discipline rules have changed, and chores have changed. They need to know that before they scold the children for something they are now allowed to do.

You may also need to renegotiate household chores again. Dave handled the finances and paying the bills when he was home, but obviously, I had to pick that up while he was gone. Was I willing to relinquish that control again when he came home?

It's also time to make new memories as a family and as a couple. When we lived in California, Michael Jackson invited returned deployees and their families to a free day at his Neverland Ranch. We had the run of the place – the zoo, the park, the movie theater, the candy store, and all the food we wanted. It was a blast. Although we never saw Michael directly, we were pretty sure he was driving around in a van with tinted windows watching us enjoy ourselves. It is a day we still remember all these years later.

Please make time to reconnect as a couple as well. When Dave came home in 2003 in California, we booked a cruise to Mexico just for us. When he came home in 1998, he and I flew to Barrow, Alaska, for one night. Both these times created new memories and new bonds for us as husband and wife.

Some base or post chapels hold pre-and post-deployment retreats to help families stay connected and bonded during the separation and to reconnect afterward.

Lessons Learned:

- *Pity parties are okay, as long as they don't last more than a day.*

- *Take advantage of opportunities to travel.*

- *Remember to pack an extra set of undergarments in your carry-on bag!*

- *Everyone changes during a deployment. Take time to get reacquainted.*

- *This too shall pass. Be patient and forgiving, and laugh a lot*

PART 5: LIVING THE LIFESTYLE

In many ways, the day-to-day life of a military spouse is the same as their civilian counterparts. You work in or out of the home. You are concerned about your children's education and health. You feel tired from handling problems at work and squabbling kids at home at the end of the day. You still cook, clean, and do laundry. The big difference is you might be doing it alone at times and in a different location every few years.

CHAPTER 15:
RAISING KIDS IN THE MILITARY

Many people think it is difficult raising children in the military, but I dispute that notion. Children are more resilient than we give them credit for, even when they are shy. My girls were shy, but they would brave the new world they found themselves in because they had each other. They made friends in the neighborhood, usually the first or second day after we moved in.

The Effects of Frequent Moves on Children

Children, of course, all react differently to moving. But in our family, the moves went smoothly. As the girls got older, we included them in deciding what bases to put on our "dream sheet." A dream sheet is where the family can list where they want to go next. (Then the assignments people laugh and send you someplace not on your list at all.)

That is how we got to Fairbanks in the first place. But in that instance, the assignments gurus knew best. We loved our new home right away, except for Alanna. She spent her first year in Alaska coming home from school, dropping her bookbag on the floor, and saying, "I hate it here. We're going sledding." Or, "I hate it here. We're going skating." And out the door, she would go. By the second year, she admitted she did like it there, and by the third year, she had just as hard a time leaving Alaska as the rest of us did at moving time.

As I said before, kids are resilient. But we as parents need to realize that they have the same feelings as we do when moving to a new base. They grieve, leaving their friends behind. They are anxious about what the new place will be like, and they are scared they will not make any friends. All we can do is reassure them what they are feeling is normal. You feel the same way too. Share your feelings with them and affirm that you will all adapt to the new surroundings together.

When you find out where your next assignment is, make it a family adventure. Research with your kids the places you can go and things you can do once you get there. That way, they have something to look forward to when you get to your new location. Then get out and explore your new area so you can become familiar with it, too.

Kids Making New Friends

Sometimes making new friends can be difficult for your children, especially if they are shy, but I can guarantee that while your child might not be part of the "in crowd" at school, they will make friends.

I remember Marissa coming home from her first day of high school and excitedly telling Alanna she made a new friend in California. They now had someone else to eat lunch with. The girls eventually had a whole posse of friends with whom they ate lunch every day. And it was really cool that their friends were from different countries around the world.

As a parent, you may need to help your child make the first move. If you moved in the summer before school starts, encourage your children to go out and play at the nearest park to meet other children in the neighborhood. Or maybe even invite a few kids to your house for a playdate or lunch. That way you can get to know the parents, too.

Sign your child up for a program at the base youth center so they can meet friends there. Enroll them in a sport they might be interested in or an art or music class. The chapel or local church is also an excellent place to meet people for everyone in the family.

I think children make friends faster than their parents do, but some kids need the extra help. Nothing says these first friends must be their best friends forever, but I know my girls are still in touch with kids from our various bases. Thanks to social media, they have located each other. Alanna and her husband, Tyler, have a mutual friend on Facebook that they did not realize the other knew. They each knew him as kids in school but on different bases. (Tyler's father also retired from the Air Force.)

Don't be afraid to encourage your children to put themselves out there, just as you must do if you want friends. Sitting in the house waiting for them to come to you just is not going to happen.

Where Will They Go to School?

The biggest concern about children in the military is where they go to school. Many parents opt to home school their children. There probably would have been a murder, suicide, or both if I had tried homeschool in our house. I was not cut out to be a teacher.

But education is a real issue in the military. Sometimes the base you are moving to is not in the best school district. When this happens, you need to decide either to homeschool, send them to private school, live on base and take your chances, or live off base in a better school district. We were lucky when we moved to our first assignment at Warner Robins AFB in Georgia. The two elementary schools on the base were part of the Department of Defense school system. Teachers fought to get jobs at those schools, and those who were hired stayed as long as they could. The schools had the reputation of having better teachers' pay than the local school districts. The children were generally better behaved than their civilian counterparts.

The girls were six years old going into first grade when we moved to Georgia. I believe they got their best education from first through third grades. The teachers maintained discipline in the classroom. They understood the emotions a military child might encounter when a parent deployed. They also understood that vacations cannot always be taken during the summers.

In Alaska, the girls went to school on base, but it was part of the Fairbanks North Star Borough. Often, we felt like the schools on the base were the last to get any money for programs, but the education was still decent.

I was most concerned about the school system in Minot, North Dakota. The girls completed their freshman year of high school in North Dakota before doing their last three years in California. In Minot, the high school did not have a consistent grading policy between departments. For example, the English department might grade on a 90-100 scale for an A, while in Science, it was 94-100. I had no problem with the stricter scale. I took issue when it came time to transfer transcripts to the new school in California. The transcripts showed the letter grade, not the percentage. When Alanna got a 92 in Science, it was a B in Minot. That brought her grade point average down when she transferred to California.

Schools across the country serving military children are developing more comprehensive systems that do not punish the military kids for how the previous school district operated. I know schools now hold tryouts for sports at the end of summer, so military kids who moved into the community can have an equal chance of making the team. I hope the transcript system changes as well.

Helping Children Cope with Deployments

The best way to help your children cope with deployments is to keep a routine. Sometimes that routine will look a little different. One parent is now doing the work of two. Keeping the routine as normal as possible is one big key to surviving the deployment.

Again, assure the kids that being sad that Daddy or Mommy is away is okay. It is okay to let those emotions out appropriately. If your child is angry at your spouse, let them verbalize that, but do not let them hit their siblings. If young children have trouble verbalizing their feelings, have them draw pictures or show how they feel through play.

When the girls were younger, they would come home from school with all sorts of pent-up emotions that they did not feel they could express during the day. Once I figured that out, I gave them 10 minutes to respectfully yell or scream about what was bothering them that day, and then they had to move on. It really worked, whether Dave was deployed or not.

Let the children share what they are feeling without demeaning them or rushing to judgment. Let them just talk. Remember, they have the same emotions you do, but they do not necessarily know how to express them appropriately. Acknowledge that you also miss Daddy or Mommy and are also counting down the days until they come home again.

Plan some special events along the way as well. The first Friday night that Dave was gone, we had a "chick flick" night. We would put on our pajamas, make some popcorn, watch movies, and sometimes sleep in the living room. I know Alanna has made special dates with her boys to go to the swimming pool or the drive-in theater near their house while Tyler was on his last deployment.

If the kids are old enough, give them responsibilities around the house. My grandsons are responsible for feeding and cleaning up after the pets. They don't always do it, and they grumble about it, but it is another distraction besides school to keep them occupied. Just as you try to stay busy, keep the children entertained as well.

You can use several methods to help your children count off the days until their deployed parent comes home, but remember that the return date can change. One of the best ideas I heard was filling a jar with Hershey's Kisses® for the number of days your spouse is supposed to be gone. The children get one Kiss a day and when the jar is empty, they know Mommy or Daddy will be home that day. I liked this approach because if your spouse is delayed in coming home, you can just add more Kisses to the jar, and the kids probably will not notice.

Whenever your spouse returns, remember your kids are trying to cope the same way you are. Acknowledge their feelings, express your own, and everyone will be happier.

Lessons Learned:

- *Children are less anxious or sad if they are active physically and mentally. Encourage them to exercise their body with outdoor games and their mind with books or puzzles. Add some of the activities to their daily routine.*

- *Children are resilient. They tend to make friends easily. Provide opportunities for them to do so.*

- *Children pick up their cues from their parents. If you are happy and excited about a move, they will be, too. If you are sad and mopey during a deployment, they will be, too.*

- *Share your feelings with your children. Be open and honest, and let them know when you are having a bad day or a good day.*

CHAPTER 16: THE MEDICAL SYSTEM

The medical system in the military is sweet, even though sometimes it can be frustrating because appointments can be hard to get. Also, doctors change frequently due to PCS or deployments. One thing to remember is you are not directly paying for it. TRICARE is the health care plan through the Department of Defense Military Health System. Initially, it covered only the military member, but it quickly evolved into the entire active-duty family system.

Suppose you are seen at a medical treatment facility (MTF), and you enroll in TRICARE prime. In that case, the cost is nothing to you for doctor visits, and prescriptions are free. Also, there is no enrollment fee for active-duty families. Retirees and others must pay an annual enrollment fee but can still get free care through an MTF on a space-available basis.

Sometimes, military families take this system for granted. For instance, I had military friends who would take their child to the pediatrician at the first sign of a cold. Since the girls were six years old when Dave came on active duty, I still remembered what it cost for a doctor visit. I often would not take them in until I felt it was necessary. Sometimes I got scolded for waiting too long.

Marissa and Mono

Occasionally, the system let me down. Appointments were not always readily available. But when that happens, you get referred to urgent care or another doctor. Remember, the MTF is first and foremost for the active-duty military member. They have priority over family members or retirees. Also, since many health care providers are active duty, they deploy too, causing shortages in the number of providers available. Mostly, the doctors, nurses, and physician assistants are competent, caring human beings.

I have two vivid memories of being disappointed by the military medical system. One incident began the week we arrived at Vandenberg Air Force Base in California, about 65 miles up the coast from Santa Barbara. We were staying in our travel trailer until we could get into our on-base house, hopefully before school started for the girls. Dave's aunt and uncle lived about three hours away, and we made plans to visit them. Daughter Marissa was not feeling well, so she stayed in the trailer. When we got home that evening, she was no better and was running a fever, which is quite unusual for her. Twin sister Alanna would run a high fever and have a cold the next day, but Marissa rarely ran a fever, so I was a little bit concerned.

After the fever persisted for four days, I decided it was time to get her to a doctor. I got an appointment for that day, and we went into the clinic. Her fever was lower but still there. She also had extremely swollen glands. After examining her, the doctor said she had a virus and prescribed ibuprofen for the aches and pains and lots of fluids, the usual treatment. But I was worried about those swollen glands. The doctor brushed me off and didn't check Marissa's glands.

We went back to the trailer, where Marissa eventually started feeling better. A week or so later, on the day we were moving into our house, Marissa complained of a sore throat. I investigated and saw that her throat was all red and covered with white dots. I was sure she had strep throat, so we went back to the clinic. A different doctor took one look at her throat, pronounced she had strep, prescribed medicine, and sent us home -- her to bed and me to finish moving in. Then she broke into a rash all over her body. She was reacting to the antibiotic, even though she had taken that medication several times before.

Another week passed. Marissa's strep throat cleared up, but she was still tired. The girls started their sophomore year of high school, and all seemed to be going well, except that Marissa would come home from school, take a two-hour nap, go to bed early, and repeat the process the next day. I finally told Dave I thought something might be wrong. She was more tired than just the typical teenage fatigue.

I started doing some research. I discovered people with mononucleosis often develop a rash when on the antibiotic prescribed for Marissa. Hmm, could she have mono? I called our primary doctor, and he examined Marissa and ran some blood tests. The result -- she had had mono but was over it.

I felt so guilty. My poor girl was sick, but I made her go to school anyway. I am the world's worst mother. But then I was angry with the first doctor we saw because if she had listened to me about Marissa's glands and did a blood test, we might have avoided all this mess in the first place.

Mothers, you know your children best, and you need to be their advocate when you know something is wrong. I should have insisted harder in Marissa's case.

Dave's Diagnosis

The second time I was let down by the military medical system was when Dave came back from East Africa in May 2011. He was fatigued and just not himself. I chalked it up to just getting home from a long deployment. But after a week, he was not much better. One morning he had bloody stools. He called the doctor, but the base hospital could not see him that day, so they referred him to an urgent-care center off base. While there, they drew some blood, and that is when our odyssey began.

A day or so later, the nurse from the urgent-care center called and told Dave he MUST stop his alcohol consumption immediately. His liver enzymes were sky-high. No matter what he said about not being a heavy drinker, she insisted he was an alcoholic in danger of losing his life. He had an appointment with his primary doctor, so he asked her to fax the lab report to his doctor.

Since we all knew he had not had any alcohol in at least eight months while deployed, we all got a good chuckle out of the nurse's warnings. Still, the enzyme levels did indicate that something was going on. The doctor ordered more blood tests and began the process of making a diagnosis.

It took many more doctors and five years to figure it out.

His doctor could not develop a definitive diagnosis. However, one test showed positive for Q-fever, a common disease around farm animals. In East Africa, the animals wander all over the place, so that could be it. Since Q-fever affects the heart, Dave was sent to a heart specialist in Oklahoma City. By the time we got to the heart doctor, the blood tests were no longer indicating Q-fever, and Dave's heart was fine.

He was tested for all types of hepatitis, some we did not even know existed, like hepatitis D and E. But none of those came back with positive results. After several months of being a pin cushion, the two-star general on the base ordered Dave to go to Brooke Army Medical Center in San Antonio, Texas.

Four months after it all started, an infectious disease doctor in San Antonio finally asked Dave about his deployment to East Africa. She asked Dave where he went, what he ate, who he encountered, and what animals and insects he came in contact with. These were all questions that should have been asked in the first place. But since it was so many months after the fact, the doctor could not determine what he was exposed to that caused his liver enzymes to spike. She sent us to a hepatologist, a doctor specializing in liver diseases, the only common denominator through all these months.

Dave was scheduled for a liver biopsy in November 2011, so we made another trip to San Antonio. He had a liver biopsy plus a colonoscopy to ensure the initial bleeding was not caused by something there. At this point, I was frustrated. I did not feel he was getting the care or the treatment he needed. I had wanted to go to San Antonio much earlier than we did. I just wanted to know what was wrong with my husband! He was tired all the time; he could not remember simple things like the name of a person he worked with every day. I did not schedule any social engagements without adding the caveat that our attendance depended on how Dave felt that day.

The first liver biopsy did not show anything conclusive. Dave's liver enzymes were coming down, so we came home and tried to live everyday life. But every time we PCS'd (military speak for a permanent reassignment), we could almost see the new doctors rubbing their hands together, wanting to be the one who solved his case. He had two more liver biopsies before doctors made a diagnosis.

We were in Ft. Lauderdale, Florida, in February 2015, so Dave could officiate at my niece's wedding when the doctor from Mississippi, where we were living, called. He needed to see Dave right away. Dave explained where we were and that we had a cruise booked for the following week. Could it wait? It turned out his enzymes had tripled from the point he had stabilized at, so the doctor needed to see him as soon as we returned.

Although not a big drinker anyway, Dave knew he couldn't drink alcohol after seeing the doctor, so like a college student trying to enjoy some adult beverages before going home, he had some cocktails at the wedding. On the cruise, he partook of the wine tasting, the whiskey tasting, the rum tasting, and any tasting he could.

Back in Mississippi, the doctor's warning was dire. "We need to take this seriously. We are playing with your life now," he said.

The doctor sent us back to San Antonio. This time the liver biopsy, Dave's third, provided a diagnosis. Dave has primary biliary cholangitis (PBC) with an overlap of autoimmune hepatitis (AIH), which attacks liver cells. The PBC is a disease that attacks the bile ducts. Both these diseases occur primarily in females. Doctors told Dave that only 5 percent of all the people with PBC are male. Also extremely uncommon is that only 7 percent of PBC patients have an overlap syndrome. He's an overachiever in my mind.

Dave's new liver specialist in St. Louis, Missouri, said the recommended treatment is based on a study of only 13 people because it is so rare, especially in men. The doctors also believe exposure to some sort of virus in East Africa triggered the autoimmune response. Still, we will never know what it was exactly.

Having a diagnosis was a great weight off our shoulders. Now we know what to expect and why Dave sometimes has bad days. PBC comes in stages like cancer. After his last biopsy, Dave was in Stage 2, but he has been holding steady since then. As he says, "Stable is good."

Lessons Learned:

• *You know your family best. Speak up and insist they get the care they need.*

• *Remember the military treatment facility is primarily for active-duty military. Your doctor may not always be available right away.*

• *Even with its shortcomings, TRICARE is still the best health care system available to military families. I'm sure many of you could say your own health plan has some shortcomings as well.*

PART 6: PROMOTIONS

Promotions are essential for all military members' careers. If you are not promoted, your career is cut short. Of course, after certain ranks, you were guaranteed a 20-year retirement. The rules have already changed since Dave's retirement with a new blended retirement system. I'm not sure how that works, so I will not get into that subject at this point.

The promotion system is different for officers and enlisted ranks. The enlisted ranks earn points for various milestones and must test for each level until they reach the senior ranks.

Officers are rated on their work and how they stack up against those going for the same rank. Promotion boards look at members' records to see what they have done and the breadth of experience they have. Then the board determines each member's potential to serve and lead in a higher rank. To make the system a little fairer, chaplains, medical officers, and lawyers do not compete against the rest of the officer corps.

This is the promotion system in an abbreviated form. It is much more complicated and changing all the time. By the time this book is published, it will have changed yet again.

Making It to The Majors

Promotion to major or technical sergeant seems to be the hardest ranks to make and the most crucial. If you make it that far, you are guaranteed a 20-year retirement from the military, not to mention the pay raises.

Dave was selected for major when we lived in North Dakota. We were confident he would make it. He was rated high among his peers and received a "definitely promote" from his commander. Those up for promotion get "racked and stacked" by their commander. This is when the base commanders name their number one, two, etc., of all the captains on base. Officers are also given "promote" or "definitely promote" if the commander feels they are among the top candidates. In this part of the process, chaplains are racked and stacked against other chaplains for the "definitely promote" designation.

As his wife, I always felt Dave was the best chaplain in the Air Force. In addition, his job as the Space Wing Chaplain was a good position for him to be in for promotion to the rank of major. So, I was confident he would clear this hurdle with no problems. Yet there was this nagging voice in the back of my mind saying, "What if he doesn't make it?"

Typically, the commander calls anyone into the office the day before the promotion list is announced if it is bad news. Dave did not get called in. He was sick at home the day the list came out, so the commander showed up at our door.

Dave came down the stairs, unshaven and in his bathrobe. He greeted the commander, a colonel, who then told him he had been selected for major and was picked as a candidate for Air Command and Staff College. Selection for the ACSC is a prestigious honor for a chaplain because only four a year were chosen to attend in person.

I threw my arms around him and congratulated him. I was so proud of him.

Later that year, rumors circulated that he was being looked at for the position of Deputy Wing Chaplain at Vandenberg Air Force Base in California. Still, Dave would not pin on his major oak leaves until after our PCS. The position was held by a Lieutenant Colonel at that time.

When we had a chaplain gathering at our house, I commented on that rumor. The Deputy Wing Chaplain's wife told me that would not happen because they would not put a new major in that position. Her husband, who had that position as a major, piped up and said, "No, Vicki's right. He is being considered for that job." A few months later, word came that Dave was selected, and we would move to California. I could not help feeling a bit smug for a day or two.

Lessons Learned:

- *The military's promotion system is complex and will differ somewhat between the various branches of service. Understanding or explaining it is nearly impossible, but it is important to the service member's career.*

- *Be your spouse's biggest cheerleader. Understand the long work hours they put in for their career. Encourage them, but don't push too hard for them to make a new rank either. Be proud of what your spouse has already done.*

CHAPTER 17: THE WAITING GAME

I wasn't worried about Dave making Lieutenant Colonel, the next rank after Major. He'd gone to Air Command and Staff College in Alabama. He then was assigned as readiness, education, and training instructor at the Chaplain Corps College. Also to his credit, Dave was moved early so he could serve as the wing chaplain at Eielson AFB in Alaska to fix a broken staff. He was filling a Lieutenant Colonel slot when he had not even met the Lieutenant Colonel selection board yet. The leadership in the chaplain corps had faith in him, and so did I.

I was most concerned about the rank of Colonel. As any good military wife, I thought my husband was the best chaplain in the entire military and more than deserved to be a colonel. However, I was worried about myself because I felt I would not be a good colonel's wife. I felt like I did when he first received his call to the ministry. He would be a good minister, but I would be a lousy minister's wife. At that time, it was because I did not sing in the choir, play piano, or teach Sunday school. Our minister's wife at that time did all three.

I had seen colonel's wives throw extravagant get-togethers and parties, and that just is not me. My idea of entertaining is hot dogs and hamburgers on the grill with my closest friends. The idea of having to open my home and serve canapes and fancy food was not in my DNA. Luckily, most of our friends enjoyed my method of entertaining.

Dave met the promotion board after our first year in Hawaii. I was sure he would make it. Dave was confident he would make it. His boss was also sure Dave would make. So, we all held our breath and waited for the big day -- the day the promotion list would come out. The wait was agonizing.

Unmet Expectations

Remember when I said the boss usually calls in the people not on the promotion list the day before to tell them the bad news? The morning before the list was made public, Dave showed up in our bedroom door in Hawaii, where I was doing some chores. I looked up.

"Hi. What are you doing home?" I asked.

"I guess I'm going to be a Lt. Col for another year," he said flatly.

It took a moment for that to sink in.

"What?"

"I did not make Colonel."

"How is that possible?" I sank down onto the bed as he crossed the room to me.

"I guess the Air Force didn't want me to be a colonel this year," he said.

We were in shock and disbelief, angry, sad, and disappointed all jumbled together. It felt like someone had died. I guess it was our dream that died. Dave's boss told him to take the rest of the day off.

"I need to get out of here. Let's go to lunch and maybe a movie," Dave suggested. I totally agreed. I wanted nothing to do with the Air Force, at least for that day.

I remembered having one thought that I verbalized.

"I don't want to be bitter about this."

We had a friend in the Air Force who did not fulfill the requirement of taking Squadron Officer School to be promoted to major. He was a good officer, but he had not put in the necessary work, even after Dave talked to him several times about it. When the Air Force implemented a reduction in force, he got caught up in it and was separated from the military. Our friend was so hurt and angry. He withdrew from anything having to do with the military or its people. We had a good life in the military. This was one setback, and I did not want to be bitter about it.

I spiraled between confusion, sadness, anger, acceptance, and back again. Dave went through the same cycle. But I also tried to look at the positives. The Air Force kept us in Hawaii for another year with the hope that Dave would make colonel with the next board, even though that rarely happens.

So, I got to stay in lovely Hawaii for another year. I got to keep the friends I had made. I had more time to explore the beautiful islands in which I lived. I did not have to move in just one year!

As a woman of faith, I knew God had a plan for Dave. God has never let us down. Yet it was frustrating not knowing God's plan for our future. Dave often asks God to make His aims known loud and clear. Was this God's call out of the Air Force chaplaincy? Life was as clear as mud, if you will excuse the cliché. All I could do was be present for Dave and wait for the next board to meet later that year.

Déjà vu: The Promotion Wait – Again

A year later in spring of 2014, we found ourselves again in the same position -- waiting to see if Dave made Colonel. We kept telling ourselves it did not matter if the board selected Dave. But it did matter. We both wanted him promoted this time. We guarded our hearts and egos against the shattering blow they took in 2013.

I still hated the waiting game. The promotion board met in November; the release date was supposed to be in early or mid-March. It seemed like such a long waiting period. Didn't they realize our military life was hanging in the balance?

Everything depended on two factors: the promotion board and the assignment people.

Dave thought we would stay in Hawaii another year, no matter the results. I liked Hawaii, but I prayed we would not remain the third year. Oh sure, it is warm and sunny all the time, and we had beautiful beaches and breathtaking mountains and blah, blah, blah.

Realistically, though, we also had 10-plus-hour plane rides to get anywhere, and they were EXPENSIVE. We had a daughter and son-in-law in Illinois and aging parents in Illinois and Wisconsin. We had friends and family on the mainland. Heck, we even had a daughter, son-in-law, and grandson living in England. Ever fly from Honolulu to London? It is not a fun, relaxing flight, and believe me, it ain't cheap.

In the end, I just hoped Dave would make colonel and then we would know our future and make plans.

Dave Is Now the Good Colonel

Phew, Dave made colonel in 2014!

Dave's boss, then Chaplain, Colonel Dondi Costin, cooked up a plot to announce his promotion. Usually, non-promotes learn their status the morning before the list becomes public to give them a chance to deal with the news. We did not hear anything on the morning of April 16, 2014. Good news? As the day dragged on, my excitement level went up.

In midafternoon, Chaplain Costin knocked on my door and said, "In 75 minutes, a car will come and get you. You will go to a room where you will wait until the appointed time. You will receive further instructions and then be escorted to a room to see Dave. Do as I told you and speak of this to no one." Of course, at that point, I knew Dave made the colonel's list.

In exactly 75 minutes (this is of course the military), the boss's wife picked me up and took me to the office next to the Command Chaplain's office. Several staff members and friends were also waiting. Waiting elsewhere, Dave was anxious because he had not heard anything and decided to go for a walk, so we had to make sure we dodged him. Chaplain Costin came in and told me the plans. He would stall in telling Dave, and then I would walk in and break the news.

Soon the Technical Sergeant came, and we followed her down the hall. She knocked on Chaplain Costin's door.

"Excuse me, do you have a counseling appointment?" she said to Dave. I was already picturing the annoyed look on his face.

"No," he said.

"Oh, because a Colonel's wife is here to see you."

At that point, I walked in.

Dave first looked exasperated and then confused -- what is my wife doing here?

"Hi, I'm a Colonel's wife," I said, throwing myself into his arms. I do not think it hit him until our friends and co-workers walked in after me.

It was priceless.

Lessons Learned:

- *Yes, military promotions are important for a service member's career, but they do NOT define or diminish that person's importance, worth, or value.*

- *Try to temper your expectations. It is hard when those expectations aren't met.*

- *Be present for your spouse if they are not promoted. Let them air their feelings, empathize with them, and let them know they still matter.*

- *Don't gloat. Be proud your spouse was promoted, but remember some people did not make the list. Sympathize with them.*

PART 7: THE END

As you near the end of your career, there are so many factors to consider. Are you retiring or separating after your stint is up? What are you and your spouse going to do after leaving the military? Do you still have children at home? Career or job? Many options will need to be explored before you make the leap out of military life. Some decisions needing to be made are the same whether you have put in four years or 20 years.

CHAPTER 18: RETIREMENT

I was tired of the military lifestyle way before Dave was. I wanted to retire after our assignment to Hawaii. We were far away from our kids, grandkids, and parents. Moving was getting to me. I just wanted to put down roots, know what my address will be in three years, and be done with the military lifestyle. However, when Dave made Colonel, we owed the Air Force three more years, one more assignment, hopefully.

Deciding When to Retire

Retirement is a problematic issue for military couples. Usually, one person wants to get out before the other, so both you and your spouse need to agree on the timing. Even though I was tired, I accepted the one last assignment to Mississippi, but then came along a second, good assignment. At the time, the Chief of Chaplains Major General Costin told the assignments board that he was sure Dave would take the position, but not so sure about me. I agreed to the additional two-year assignment to Virginia, after which Dave would only have seven months left before he would be forced out due to his age.

Dave wanted to go out on his own terms, so he wanted to retire before he was told. I remember one morning, he rolled over in bed and said, "September 1, 2018."

"What's September 1, 2018?"

"That's my retirement date."

Okay. Now I knew. We could start making plans, and I had something concrete to look forward to.

Circumstances led to Dave retiring as of July 1, 2018. He said it felt like moving up his retirement date was the right thing to do. It allowed us to move into our house in Illinois earlier so it would not sit empty for so long, and it also allowed us to take our trip to the northeast in 2018. As for the

Air Force, it allowed Dave's vacant position to be filled during the regular summer PCS cycle.

In the military, if you have any leave time accrued at the end of the year, a lot of military members use it up before their retirement date. Even though Dave's official date was July 1, he finished working at the end of April 2018. That gave us time to move into our home in Illinois and take a trip while he still had active-duty pay coming in.

Deciding Where to Retire

We were lucky we already had a place to live in retirement. Many couples do not know where they are going or what they will be doing when the retirement question comes up. That is another question you must discuss. Where are you going to live?

In 2012, we decided we wanted to live near our daughter in central Illinois and bought a house with that in mind. Throughout his military career, Dave always said he did not want to live in Illinois, but I still felt it would be best to come back to our roots.

The biggest considerations in deciding where to live include the job market, available healthcare, schools, and nearness to family.

Does your military spouse want another career after getting out of the service? Dave and I tossed several ideas around. First, we thought he could help a small church that could not afford a full-time pastor. We would not need a salary because of his retirement pay. We would not need to find new health insurance because we would both continue to be covered under TRICARE, the military insurance.

Dave also thought about being a police or fire department chaplain. He loved working with first responders and people in uniform, and he could do that on a volunteer basis if need be.

He ended up going with the first choice as part-time pastor of a small rural church about 35 miles from our home. He enjoys the work, and it fulfills a need for both the church and Dave. Plus, it keeps him out of my hair, which was my main concern about retiring.

What Will Retirement Look Like?

You also will need to determine what retirement will look like for you and your family. Do you want to travel? Do you want to be free to watch the grandkids or your own kids if they are still home? After leaving the military life, do you want the opportunity to explore your own interests after all those years of putting them on hold?

Believe it or not, we both had concerns about whether we would be able to live in one place for more than three years. As of this writing, we have made it two-and-a-half years without twitching too much, but the summer of 2021 will be three years. We do not know how we will respond at that point. But I do know we are not planning on moving again until the children put us in a retirement community.

Because we moved so often, 14 times for the military and a total of 18 times since we were married, we joke about not cleaning the windows because when it was time to do so, we moved. Or not wholly organizing things because we will do it when we move. On the other hand, we do not have a lot of clutter because we cleaned out extraneous items before each move. Now we are faced with having to deal with dirty windows and organizing the house to keep it uncluttered.

I know one activity we will continue to do is traveling. We enjoy camping in our travel trailer and going on cruises. We will keep going on trips as long as we are physically able.

Whatever your time after the military looks like, enjoy it. Do what you want to do. Start that dream business or the career you have always wanted. Make new friends you will not have to leave in a few years. Draw on the strength you have developed as a military spouse to design your dream life.

Lessons Learned:

- *You have had to make many decisions throughout your military life. But the decisions you will make when you leave that life behind are just as important.*

- *Start planning at least a year before retirement. Ask all your important questions early so you have a plan in place when the day comes.*

- *Don't jump into a new job or career right away. Take some time to relax, adjust to your new circumstances, and familiarize yourself with your surroundings.*

AFTERWORD

Dave retired in July 2018, and we moved back to central Illinois to be near Marissa, Andy, and their girls. Retirement is different, but we are adjusting. In addition to Dave serving as the part-time pastor for the Crow Meadow Presbyterian Church in La Rose, Illinois, he also accepted a position on the Commission on Ministry for our Presbytery. He served part-time for six months at First Presbyterian Church in Normal, Illinois, where I am a member. Dave joined the local VFW Post and became organizing secretary for the State of Illinois of the Military Order of Foreign Wars. He officially "failed" retirement, but I cannot see my organized, disciplined, Type-A husband sitting around doing nothing.

After our household goods were delivered in May 2018, we took off in our travel trailer to explore the United States and Canada's northeast portion. Neither of us had been to Vermont, the only state of the 50 we had not visited, so the goal was to stop in Vermont on our way to Nova Scotia in Canada. On the road, we visited with several retired military friends and attended another friend's retirement party in Ohio. We planned to be on the road for about two months. We made it five-and-a-half weeks before we were tired and needed to go home again.

We enjoyed traveling whenever and wherever we wanted until COVID-19 stopped that in 2020. We still took the trailer out and discovered if we went during the week and came home on weekends, the parks were not too crowded. We visit with Alanna, Tyler, and the boys a couple times a year now that they live in Delaware instead of England. Nearer to home, we get to play with our two granddaughters frequently since they literally live around the corner from us.

As of this writing, Dave's health continues to hold steady, which is okay with us. We have some cruising to do and another long camping trip to take before we are ready to stop traversing the globe.

I sometimes dream about our time in the Air Force, and I miss it a lot. But I still stay in touch with many friends from all our time served. I am not so far removed, and I do still have the means to get information about the military.

I hope you found my book and stories helpful and inspiring. Living in the military certainly has its challenges. Remember many spouses have paved the road before you, and you, in turn, can help make the way smoother for the next generation. It's a great way of life. I know you can thrive in it. I believe in you.

APPENDIX I: ACRONYMS & ABBREVIATIONS YOU NEED TO KNOW

The military is full of acronyms and abbreviations, and even after 31 years, I still did not know what half of them were. It seems each branch of service and each base have their own. So here is a list of essential acronyms and abbreviations you will want and need to know, courtesy of Military OneSource. (www.militaryonesource.mil)

The Basics

- **AAFES:** Army and Air Force Exchange Service. The retailer that operates post exchanges on Army and Air Force installations. In the Navy, it is the Navy Exchange, or NEX. You will hear it referred to as the PX (Post Exchange) on Army Posts and the BX (Base Exchange) on Air Force Bases.

- **AIT or "A School":** Advanced individual training. The hands-on career training and field instruction each service member receives before being qualified to do a specific military job. This specialized schooling varies by military branch.

- **ASVAB:** Armed Services Vocational Aptitude Battery. A multiple-choice test that all prospective recruits take before enlisting to see if they are qualified to join and which military jobs they qualify for.

- **DOD:** Department of Defense. The department of the U.S. government responsible for military operations.

- **MEPS:** Military Entrance Processing Station. The place where service members take the ASVAB, get a physical, choose their military job, and are sworn into military service.

111

- **MOS:** Military occupational specialty. This is a service member's specific job in the military, from artillery and aviation to engineering and intelligence. The Air Force calls this the Air Force Specialty Code, or **AFSC**.

- **OPSEC:** Operational Security. The process of identifying and protecting information about military operations.

- **PT:** Physical training. Critical to military readiness. Service members will be expected to meet fitness standards throughout their enlistment.

Chain of Command

- **CO:** Commanding officer, or **CC:** Company Commander. The officer in charge of a military unit, such as captain for a company (Army) and squadron commander for a squadron of aircraft (Air Force).

- **JCS:** Joint Chiefs of Staff. A group of senior military leaders from each military branch advises the president, the Secretary of Defense, the Homeland Security Council, and the National Security Council on military matters.

- **NCO:** Noncommissioned officer. A military officer who has not received a commission, such as sergeant (Army and Air Force) and warrant officer (Navy).

- **XO:** Executive officer. The second-in-command to a commanding officer.

Important Paperwork

- **BRS:** Blended Retirement System. The military's new retirement system extends benefits to about 85% of service members, even if they do not serve a full 20 years. This system uses the Thrift Savings Plan (TSP) described below.

- **DEERS:** Defense Enrollment Eligibility Reporting System. A database of military families and others entitled to receive TRICARE and other benefits.

- **LES:** Leave and Earning Statement. This bimonthly statement reports what you have earned, how much has been withheld for taxes, your leave balance, and what automatic payments you have. Service members in the Air Force or Army may choose to receive their pay monthly rather than biweekly, in which case the LES would be reported only once a month instead of twice.

- **POC:** Point of contact. The person you contact about a specific program or assignment.

- **TRICARE:** Military health care program. TRICARE provides health benefits to service members, retirees, and their families.

TSP: Thrift Savings Plan. Like a 401(k), the TSP is a government-sponsored retirement saving and investment plan. The TSP is a fundamental part of the military's new Blended Retirement System (BRS), described above.

Financial and Housing

- **BAH:** Basic Allowance for Housing. Compensation that service members receive to help cover the cost of housing when government quarters are not provided.

- **COLA:** Cost of Living Allowance. Compensation that service members receive to offset the cost of living in more expensive areas of the U.S.

- **OHA:** Overseas Housing Allowance. Compensation that service members receive for housing outside the U.S. when government quarters are not available.

- **POC:** Privately Owned Conveyance. A service member's personal vehicle is not owned by the government. Also referred to as a personally owned vehicle (POV).

Locations

- **ACSC:** Air Command and Staff College. A school in the Air Force needed to be considered for the rank of Lieutenant Colonel.

- **CONUS/OCONUS:** The continental U.S., or CONUS, is the 48 contiguous states and the District of Columbia. OCONUS is outside the continental U.S., including Alaska and Hawaii.

- **DITY:** Do-It-Yourself, or a personally procured move, can save a service member a lot of money in moving expenses. This is often associated with moving during a permanent change of station (PCS).

- **FOB:** Forward operating base. A temporary, secured operational position that supports strategic goals and tactical objectives.

- **MTF:** Military treatment facility. A healthcare center for active-duty military, their families, and retirees.

- **PCS:** Permanent change of station. The relocation of an active-duty service member to a different duty location. Service members may PCS every few years.

- **PPM:** Personally procured move. A move that a service member plans and conducts on their own instead of having the military do it. PPM expenses may be reimbursed by the military.

- **TDY:** Temporary duty station. A temporary assignment at a location other than a service member's permanent duty station.

- **TLF:** Temporary lodging facility. Temporary housing where military members and their families can stay on-base while waiting to get permanent housing either on-base or off-base.

Social

- **A&FRC:** Airmen and Family Readiness Center. A center to help Air Force families prepare for moves, deployments, and other activities. They often hold classes on finance, parenting, etc.

- **ESC:** Enlisted Spouse Club. A philanthropic and social group for enlisted military spouses.

- **FRG:** Family Readiness Group. Offers the same services as the A&FRC but on Army Posts.

- **Ombudsmen:** Same as above but for the Navy.

- **OSC:** Officers' Spouse Club. A philanthropic and social group of officer spouses raising money for scholarships. Many ESC and OSC groups are combining to form one Spouse Club.

- **SC:** What combined spouse clubs are called.

APPENDIX II – ONLINE & ON-BASE RESOURCES TO HELP YOU

Online Resources:

- **Military One Source:** The go-to resource for everything military. On this site, you can find the answer to just about any question about deployments, employment, caring for children, information on bases and posts, family life, financial counseling, and mental health counseling. www.militaryonesource.mil

- **Military.com:** Another good clearinghouse for information on everything military. This site has information on family life, benefits, education, relationships, Permanent Change of Station, and career advancement potential. You can also select a branch of the military for information specific to that branch. www.military.com

- **Military Spouse Jobs:** This site offers 1-on-1 job placement support. They also work with you to explore different career options and training, all at no cost to the spouse or the employers. For Active Duty, Reserves, or National Guard spouses. www.militaryspousejobs.org

- **Military Spouse Preference Program:** A program that gives military spouses preference when filling a job on base. https://www.dcpas.osd.mil/

- **TRICARE:** On this site, you can find medical information including different TRICARE plans, how to find a doctor, booking appointments, and viewing your health record. www.tricare.mil

- **Military Benefits:** Information on some of the top benefits for military spouses including the Military Spouse Career Advancement Account (MyCAA) program, Transferred GI Bill® Benefits,

Military Spouse Preference Program, scholarships, military discounts, military lodging, hotels, and travel, and a myriad of other benefits. https://militarybenefits.info/

Local /On-base Resources:

- **Family Resource Centers**
- **Chaplains' Office**
- **Housing Office**
- **Maintenance Office**
- **Key Spouse or Ombudsman**
- **First Sergeant**
- **Spouse Clubs**
- **Legal Office**
- **Military Family Life Counselor**

This resource list is not intended to be all-inclusive for every branch of service. When in doubt about who to call, start with the **Family Resource Center**. They can guide you in the right direction. You can also Google what you need help with to see other resources available to help you with your problem or situation.

Acknowledgments

I would like to acknowledge the following people without whom this book would not be possible.

My husband, Dave, for taking me on this journey around the world.

For my daughters, Marissa and Alanna, for being the best "military brats" in the world!

For Denise Jones, my long-time friend, and editor for making this book readable.

For Amy, a new military spouse who took the time to give me her take on the book.

For the gang at Self-Publishing School, especially Dillon and Josiah, who convinced me the school would be the best investment in myself, and Sloane and Ellaine, my coaches who encouraged me every step of the way. Thanks for the kick in the rear to get me going.

Self-Publishing School

NOW IT'S YOUR TURN

Discover the EXACT 3-step blueprint you need to become a bestselling author in as little as 3 months.

Self-Publishing School helped me, and now I want them to help you with this FREE resource to begin outlining your book!

Even if you're busy, bad at writing, or don't know where to start, you CAN write a bestseller and build your best life.

With tools and experience across a variety of niches and professions, Self-Publishing School is the <u>only</u> resource you need to take your book to the finish line!

DON'T WAIT

Say "YES" to becoming a bestseller:

https://self-publishingschool.com/friend/

Follow the steps on the page to get a FREE resource to get started on your book and unlock a discount to get started with Self-Publishing School

ABOUT THE AUTHOR

Victoria Terrinoni is an author, freelance writer, blogger, and wife of a retired Air Force Chaplain, who served for 31 years. She is also a mother of twin daughters, mother-in-law to two great sons-in-law and a Nonna to four "perfect" grandchildren.

Can You Help?

Thank You for Reading My Book!

Please leave me an honest review on Amazon
letting me know what you thought of the book.

Thanks so much!

Victoria Terrinoni

Made in the USA
Columbia, SC
18 August 2021